Keto Meal Prep

70+ Quick and Easy Low Carb Keto Recipes to Burn Fat and Lose Weight & Simple, Proven Intermittent Fasting Guide for Beginners

By

Mark Evans

© **Copyright 2018 by Mark Evans**

All rights reserved.

The following book is reproduced below with the goal of providing information that is as accurate and as reliable as possible. Regardless, purchasing this book can be seen as consent to the fact that both the publisher and the author of this book are in no way experts on the topics discussed within, and that any recommendations or suggestions made herein are for entertainment purposes only. Professionals should be consulted as needed before undertaking any of the action endorsed herein.

This declaration is deemed fair and valid by both the American Bar Association and the Committee of Publishers Association and is legally binding throughout the United States.

Furthermore, the transmission, duplication or reproduction of any of the following work, including precise information, will be considered an illegal act, irrespective whether it is done electronically or in print. The legality extends to creating a secondary or tertiary copy of the work or a recorded copy and is only allowed with express written consent of the Publisher. All additional rights are reserved.

The information in the following pages is broadly considered to be a truthful and accurate account of facts, and as such any inattention, use or misuse of the information in question by the reader will render any resulting actions solely under their purview. There are no scenarios in which the publisher or the original author of this work can be in any fashion deemed liable for any hardship or damages that may befall them after undertaking information described herein.

Additionally, the information found on the following pages is intended for informational purposes only and should thus be considered, universal. As befitting its nature, the information presented is without assurance regarding its continued validity or interim quality. Trademarks that mentioned are done without written consent and can in no way be considered an endorsement from the trademark holder.

All additional rights reserved.

Table of Contents

Book – I: Meal Prep: Beginner's Guide to 70+ Quick and Easy Low Carb Keto Recipes to Burn Fat and Lose Weight Fast

Chapter 1 – The Basics and Benefits of Low Carb Keto Meal Prepping 6

Chapter 2 – 30-Day Low Carb Keto Meal Plan 10

Chapter 3 – Keto Meal Prep Breakfast Recipes 41

Chapter 4 – Keto Meal Prep Lunch Recipes 65

Chapter 5 – Keto Meal Prep Dinner Recipes 95

Chapter 6 – Keto Meal Prep Snack Recipes 119

Chapter 7 – Keto Meal Prep Smoothie Recipes 151

Chapter 8 – Keto Meal Prep Dessert Recipes 171

Conclusion 185

Book – II: INTERMITTENT FASTING: A Simple, Proven Approach to the Intermittent Fasting Lifestyle - Burn Fat, Build Muscle, Eat What You Want

Introduction 188

Part I – Everything You Need to Know About Intermittent Fasting 189

Part II – Comprehensive Guide to Intermittent Fasting 212

Part III – Supplemental Section 226

Conclusion 240

Keto Meal Prep

Book - I

Meal Prep

Beginner's Guide to 70+ Quick and Easy Low Carb Keto Recipes to burn Fat and Lose Weight Fast

Chapter 1 – The Basics and Benefits of Low Carb Keto Meal Prepping

The Ketogenic Diet, or Keto, is fast becoming the alternative diet for many people. It has helped many lose weight, overcome PCOS (polycystic ovarian syndrome), enhance their athletic performance, and manage Alzheimer's disease and other neurological conditions.

If you are someone who is currently on the Keto diet, then you would understand how difficult it can be to maintain, especially since we are often surrounded by high carb food. Keto dieters more often than not would need to prepare their own meals at home to ensure their enjoyment of delicious, healthy, low carb and high fat food.

The good news, however, is that you can choose to **meal prep** your low carb keto meals. That way, can save a lot of money, time, and effort as you continue to be on the keto diet. Meal prepping is a practical way to prepare food at home because it enables you to cook large batches for only a few times per week (sometimes even once a week) and then store individual portions of the food properly in the refrigerator or freezer. Then, throughout the week, all you will have to do is reheat those servings and enjoy them. Best of all, some foods, such as salads and snacks, do not even need reheating at all.

How to Meal Prep the Right Way

Some people have quit meal prepping simply because they do not follow a practical and efficient process. You can avoid becoming one of them by creating one, and these guidelines can help you do so.

1: Choose where and when to do your weekly grocery shopping
Where would you like to buy your ingredients? Take note of the closest markets in your area that offer the best quality your food budget can afford. Then, determine the best day and time to purchase all the ingredients you need there. For instance, if your free day is on a Saturday

morning and you know not a lot of people do their grocery shopping at 10 a.m. in that market, then you can schedule your weekly trips then.

2: Create a grocery list template.

Whether it is on your phone or a physical list, you should have a template on which to list down the ingredients you need for the recipes you will be meal prepping. Take note of the amount, generic names, and brands if you must. Then, sit down with your chosen recipes for the week and take note.

3: Shop in bulk.

Once you have a list of the ingredients you need, all you have to do is buy them during your chosen date and time. Then, store them appropriately in your kitchen pantry and refrigerator as soon as you get home.

4: Choose two Meal Prep Days.

Before you go grocery shopping, make sure you have already chosen your meal prep day for the week. Is it going to be on a Sunday afternoon? If so, then make sure you have bought the ingredients a day before. That way, you will not be so exhausted by the time you start cooking.

5: Prepare your individual food containers.

You will make your own life so much easier if you divide your meal prepped meals into individual containers because you will then be able to do a "grab and go" system throughout the week. Choose guaranteed food-safe, airtight containers suitable for the types of foods you want to enjoy. Also, label the containers so you would not end up storing your delicate muffins in one that smells strongly of garlic and pepper.

There you have it: meal prepping made easy. If you are not the only one who will enjoy these meal prepped meals, then you can definitely work together with whoever you are sharing them with. That way, you can cut on cost and time so much more effectively.

Common Mistakes in Meal Prepping

There are definitely safety measures to take when meal prepping. After all, you are dealing with something that you put into your body. So, here are some common mistakes you must avoid while meal prepping your low carb Keto meals.

Mistake 1: Storing cooked food for more than 4 days in the fridge.

The safest maximum number of days for storing most cooked food in the refrigerator (40 degrees F or lower) is 4 days. The food should also be stored in an airtight container to significantly slow down oxidation. Any longer than 4 days and you might risk food poisoning.

Mistake 2: Reheating food more than once

Cooked food should never be reheated more than once. Otherwise, you could risk not just losing the nutritional value and flavor but also the chance of food poisoning. You should also reheat the food until the internal temperature reaches 165 degrees F to ensure that it is completely thawed and safe to eat.

Mistake 3: Going to the grocery store without a detailed list

You could waste a lot of money and food when you overbuy certain ingredients. It is therefore critical for you to take note of the amount required for the meal prep before you step into the grocery store.

Mistake 4: Storing food improperly

Oxygen quickly breaks down the food and causes bacteria to flourish, that is why you must minimize the food's exposure to oxygen as soon as it is cool enough to be stored. This can be achieved by using airtight containers and freezer bags. You can also do the water immersion technique to make bagged food airtight before sealing. Check any online video on how to do this.

Mistake 5: Failing to add variety

It is important to eat different food within the week for two reasons. First is, you could easily grow bored with the same meals every day. Second is, you will not be able to give your body a variety of nutrients if you eat the same types of food daily. So, do not hesitate to try other recipes. Better yet, always include a fresh salad with most of your meals so you will not only add variety to flavor, but also to nutrients.

At this point, you must be ready to start low carb Keto meal prepping. So, without further ado, go ahead and get started!

Chapter 2 – 30-Day Low Carb Keto Meal Plan

In the following pages is a suggested 30-day list of meal plans you can follow, based on the recipes found in this book. Of course, you can always make changes based on your personal taste and preferences, so feel free to adjust when needed.

Day 1

Breakfast: Savory Cheddar Pancakes

Smoothie: Creamy Matcha Green Tea Smoothie

Lunch: Savory Beef Balls with Asian Style Dip

Snacks: Avocado, Cream Cheese and Cucumber Bites

Dinner: Deviled Eggs with Chopped Bacon

Dessert: Cocoa Nibbles with Cream Cheese

Day 2

Breakfast: Savory Cheddar Pancakes

Smoothie: Creamy Matcha Green Tea Smoothie

Lunch: Savory Beef Balls with Asian Style Dip

Snacks: Avocado, Cream Cheese and Cucumber Bites

Dinner: Deviled Eggs with Chopped Bacon

Dessert: Cocoa Nibbles with Cream Cheese

Day 3

Breakfast: Chia Cinnamon Vanilla Granola

Smoothie: Peanut Butter Choco Smoothie

Lunch: Savory Beef Balls with Asian Style Dip

Snacks: Avocado, Cream Cheese and Cucumber Bites

Dinner: Keto Caesar Salad

Dessert: Cocoa Nibbles with Cream Cheese

Day 4

Breakfast: Chia Cinnamon Vanilla Granola

Smoothie: Peanut Butter Choco Smoothie

Lunch: Chicken Curry with Oil-Roasted Peanuts

Snacks: Ham 'n' Cheese Puffs

Dinner: Keto Caesar Salad

Dessert: Creamy Vanilla Pudding

Day 5

Breakfast: Chia Cinnamon Vanilla Granola

Smoothie: Strawberries and Cream Smoothie

Lunch: Chicken Curry with Oil-Roasted Peanuts

Snacks: Ham 'n' Cheese Puffs

Dinner: Fried Cheesy Avocado Wedges

Dessert: Creamy Vanilla Pudding

Day 6

Breakfast: Cheese and Sausage in Portobello Breakfast Burgers

Smoothie: Strawberries and Cream Smoothie

Lunch: Baked Parmesan Chicken Nuggets in Mozzarella Marinara Sauce

Snacks: Ham 'n' Cheese Puffs

Dinner: Fried Cheesy Avocado Wedges

Dessert: Creamy Vanilla Pudding

Day 7

Breakfast: Cheese and Sausage in Portobello Breakfast Burgers

Smoothie: Zesty Green Smoothie

Lunch: Baked Parmesan Chicken Nuggets in Mozzarella Marinara Sauce

Snacks: Walnut Parmesan Bites

Dinner: Simple Beef Chili

Dessert: Lemon Poppy Seed Cupcakes

Day 8

Breakfast: Cheesy Keto Quiche

Smoothie: Zesty Green Smoothie

Lunch: Zucchini Beef Lasagna

Snacks: Walnut Parmesan Bites

Dinner: Simple Beef Chili

Dessert: Lemon Poppy Seed Cupcakes

Day 9

Breakfast: Cheesy Keto Quiche

Smoothie: Chia Seeds and Crisp Greens Smoothie

Lunch: Zucchini Beef Lasagna

Snacks: Walnut Parmesan Bites

Dinner: Low Carb Hearty Pot Roast

Dessert: Lemon Poppy Seed Cupcakes

Day 10

Breakfast: Blueberry Breakfast Scones

Smoothie: Chia Seeds and Crisp Greens Smoothie

Lunch: Chicken Bell Pepper Kebabs

Snacks: Cream Cheese Bacon Stuffed Jalapenos

Dinner: Low Carb Hearty Pot Roast

Dessert: Keto Choco Brownies

Day 11

Breakfast: Blueberry Breakfast Scones

Smoothie: Buttered Coffee Smoothie

Lunch: Chicken Bell Pepper Kebabs

Snacks: Cream Cheese Bacon Stuffed Jalapenos

Dinner: Miso Beef and Tender Zucchini

Dessert: Keto Choco Brownies

Day 12

Breakfast: Cinnamon Coconut Porridge

Smoothie: Buttered Coffee Smoothie

Lunch: Chicken Bell Pepper Kebabs

Snacks: Cream Cheese Bacon Stuffed Jalapenos

Dinner: Miso Beef and Tender Zucchini

Dessert: Keto Choco Brownies

Day 13

Breakfast: Cinnamon Coconut Porridge

Smoothie: Smooth Vanilla Smoothie

Lunch: Easy Grilled Shrimp with Avocado, Tomato and Onion Salad

Snacks: Low Carb Guacamole

Dinner: Roasted Garlic Butter Cod with Bok Choy

Dessert: No Bake Coconut Macaroons

Day 14

Breakfast: Easy Scotch Eggs

Smoothie: Smooth Vanilla Smoothie

Lunch: Easy Grilled Shrimp with Avocado, Tomato and Onion Salad

Snacks: Low Carb Guacamole

Dinner: Roasted Garlic Butter Cod with Bok Choy

Dessert: No Bake Coconut Macaroons

Day 15

Breakfast: Easy Scotch Eggs

Smoothie: Avocado Coco Smoothie

Lunch: Mediterranean Style Tuna Salad

Snacks: Low Carb Guacamole

Dinner: Creamy Chicken Soup

Dessert: No Bake Coconut Macaroons

Day 16

Breakfast: Easy Scotch Eggs

Smoothie: Avocado Coco Smoothie

Lunch: Mediterranean Style Tuna Salad

Snacks:

Dinner: Creamy Chicken Soup

Dessert: Raspberry Cream Cheese Pops

Day 17

Breakfast: Easy Breakfast Tacos

Smoothie: Creamy Matcha Green Tea Smoothie

Lunch: Creamy Cauli Mac 'n' Cheese

Snacks: Smoked Salmon and Dill Spread

Dinner: Ginger Sesame Halibut

Dessert: Raspberry Cream Cheese Pops

Day 18

Breakfast: Easy Breakfast Tacos

Smoothie: Creamy Matcha Green Tea Smoothie

Lunch: Creamy Cauli Mac 'n' Cheese

Snacks: Smoked Salmon and Dill Spread

Dinner: Ginger Sesame Halibut

Dessert: Raspberry Cream Cheese Pops

Day 19

Breakfast: Bacon and Ricotta Breakfast Muffins

Smoothie: Peanut Butter Choco Smoothie

Lunch: Balsamic Herbed Pork Tenderloin

Snacks: Smoked Salmon and Dill Spread

Dinner: Hearty Beef and Mushroom Stew

Dessert: Coco Peanut Butter Bites

Day 20

Breakfast: Bacon and Ricotta Breakfast Muffins

Smoothie: Peanut Butter Choco Smoothie

Lunch: Balsamic Herbed Pork Tenderloin

Snacks: Coco Lime Fat Bombs

Dinner: Hearty Beef and Mushroom Stew

Dessert: Coco Peanut Butter Bites

Day 21

Breakfast: Bacon and Ricotta Breakfast Muffins

Smoothie: Strawberries and Cream Smoothie

Lunch: Sardine and Garden Salad

Snacks: Coco Lime Fat Bombs

Dinner: Goat Cheese and Smoked Onion Pizza

Dessert: Coco Peanut Butter Bites

Day 22

Breakfast: Keto Mini Waffles

Smoothie: Strawberries and Cream Smoothie

Lunch: Sardine and Garden Salad

Snacks: Coco Lime Fat Bombs

Dinner: Goat Cheese and Smoked Onion Pizza

Dessert: Cocoa Nibbles with Cream Cheese

Day 23

Breakfast: Keto Mini Waffles

Smoothie: Zesty Green Smoothie

Lunch: Herbed Parmesan Chicken Fingers

Snacks: Coco Lemon Fat Bombs

Dinner: Savory Butternut Squash Soup

Dessert: Cocoa Nibbles with Cream Cheese

Day 24

Breakfast: Bacon and Ricotta Breakfast Muffins

Smoothie: Zesty Green Smoothie

Lunch: Herbed Parmesan Chicken Fingers

Snacks: Coco Lemon Fat Bombs

Dinner: Savory Butternut Squash Soup

Dessert: Cocoa Nibbles with Cream Cheese

Day 25

Breakfast: Bacon and Ricotta Breakfast Muffins

Smoothie: Chia Seeds and Crisp Greens Smoothie

Lunch: Ham, Onion and Green Bean Salad

Snacks: Coco Lemon Fat Bombs

Dinner: Savory Butternut Squash Soup

Dessert: Creamy Vanilla Pudding

Day 26

Breakfast: Creamy Herbed Baked Eggs

Smoothie: Chia Seeds and Crisp Greens Smoothie

Lunch: Ham, Onion and Green Bean Salad

Snacks: Roasted Eggplant Spread

Dinner: Deviled Eggs with Chopped Bacon

Dessert: Creamy Vanilla Pudding

Day 27

Breakfast: Creamy Herbed Baked Eggs

Smoothie: Smooth Vanilla Smoothie

Lunch: Cheesy Avocado Beef Patties

Snacks: Choco Peanut Fat Bombs

Dinner: Deviled Eggs with Chopped Bacon

Dessert: Creamy Vanilla Pudding

Day 28

Breakfast: Keto Bread and Cinnamon Butter

Smoothie: Smooth Vanilla Smoothie

Lunch: Cheesy Avocado Beef Patties

Snacks: Cauli Cheddar Bites

Dinner: Deviled Eggs with Chopped Bacon

Dessert: Lemon Poppy Seed Cupcakes

Day 29

Breakfast: Keto Bread and Cinnamon Butter

Smoothie: Avocado Coco Smoothie

Lunch: Cheesy Sausage, Mushroom and Spaghetti Squash Casserole

Snacks: Cauli Cheddar Bites

Dinner: Keto Caesar Salad

Dessert: Lemon Poppy Seed Cupcakes

Day 30

Breakfast: Keto Bread and Cinnamon Butter

Smoothie: Avocado Coco Smoothie

Lunch: Cheesy Sausage, Mushroom and Spaghetti Squash Casserole

Snacks: Cauli Cheddar Bites

Dinner: Keto Caesar Salad

Dessert: Lemon Poppy Seed Cupcakes

Chapter 3 – Keto Meal Prep Breakfast Recipes

Recipe #1: Savory Cheddar Pancakes

Number of Servings: 4
Serving Size: 2 pancakes

Prep Time: 15 minutes
Cook Time: 10 minutes

Ingredients:

- 4 large egg whites
- 4 oz. grated cheddar cheese
- 2 cups almond meal
- 4 Tbsp. olive oil
- 1 Tbsp. chopped green onion
- 1 tsp. baking powder

Cooking Directions:

1. Combine the almond meal, water, grated cheddar cheese, green onion, and garlic in a large bowl. Mix well and set aside.
2. Whisk the egg whites in a separate bowl together with the baking powder, then add the almond meal mixture. Beat everything well until smooth.
3. Place a pancake griddle or nonstick skillet over medium high flame and heat through. Add a bit of the olive oil and swirl to coat.

4. Once hot, ladle in an eighth of the batter into the hot skillet and cook for 1 minute per side, or until set.

5. Transfer to a platter then repeat with the remaining batter. Place in an airtight container and refrigerate for up to 3 days. Reheat before serving.

Nutritional Facts per Serving:

Energy (calories)	257	kcal
Protein	11	g
Fat	24	g
Net Carbohydrates	2	g
Fiber	0.1	g
Sugars, total	0.4	g

Recipe #2: Chia Cinnamon Vanilla Granola

Number of Servings: 6
Serving Size: ½ cup

Prep Time: 20 minutes
Cook Time: 25 minutes

Ingredients:

- 56 grams whey protein powder
- 1 cup macadamia nuts
- ¼ cup water
- 4 Tbsp. flaxseed meal
- 4 Tbsp. whole chia seeds
- 4 Tbsp. coconut oil, melted
- 3 Tbsp. water
- 4 tsp. stevia
- 2 tsp. cinnamon
- 1 tsp. pure vanilla extract
- ¼ tsp. fine sea salt

Cooking Directions:

1. Set the oven to 350 degrees F to preheat. Line a baking sheet with baking paper and set aside.

2. Mix together the vanilla extract, water, and chia seeds in a large bowl. Set aside for 5 minutes, or until the mixture becomes gelatinous.

3. Pour the macadamia nuts into a food processor then add the flaxseed meal, protein powder, stevia, salt, and cinnamon. Pulse until the mixture is fine and the nuts are grounded.

4. Pour the gelatinous chia seed mixture into the food processor, then add about 1 ½ tablespoons of water and the coconut oil. Blend until the mixture is smooth. Set aside.

5. Using a tablespoon, transfer the mixture onto the prepared baking sheet. Then, transfer to the oven and bake for 15 minutes.

6. Once baked, remove from the oven and break into small pieces. Spread out on the pan.

7. Bake for an additional 10 minutes, or until the granola is dry and golden brown. Set on a cooling rack and allow to cool completely.

8. Transfer to an airtight container and store for up to 1 week in the refrigerator. Best served with warm milk.

Nutritional Facts per Serving:

Energy (calories)	336	kcal
Protein	9	g
Fat	31	g
Net Carbohydrates	11	g
Fiber	6	g
Sugars, total	1.3	g

Recipe #3: Cheese and Sausage in Portobello Breakfast Burgers

Number of Servings: 4
Serving Size: 1 patty

Prep Time: 25 minutes
Cook Time: 20 minutes

Ingredients:
- 8 Portobello mushroom caps
- 4 slices American cheese, 2 oz. each
- ¼ cup breakfast sausage
- 4 Tbsp. olive oil

Cooking Directions:

1. Rinse the mushroom caps thoroughly, removing and discarding the stems and gills. Blot dry with paper towels and set aside.

2. Place a large cast iron skillet over medium flame and heat through. Once hot, add a quarter of the olive oil and swirl to coat.

3. Add two of the Portobello mushroom caps and cook for 5 minutes per side, or until browned all over. Transfer to a platter and repeat with the remaining mushroom caps. Set aside.

4. Divide the breakfast sausage into four patties.

5. Wipe the skillet clean and reheat over medium flame. Add half of the remaining olive oil and swirl to coat. Add two of the patties and cook for about 2 to 3 minutes per side, or until cooked through.

6. Add a slice of American cheese on each patty, then cover the pan and cook until the cheese is melted.

7. Slice the patties with the melted cheese into the mushroom caps. Repeat with the remaining patties and cheese slices until four patties have patties.

8. Cover the top of the mushroom caps with the other patties until you have four "burgers."

9. Wrap each "burger" in aluminum foil and refrigerate for up to 3 days, or freeze for up to 3 weeks. Reheat before serving.

Nutritional Facts per Serving:

Energy (calories)	504	kcal
Protein	24	g
Fat	41	g
Net Carbohydrates	10	g
Fiber	3	g
Sugars, total	7	g

Recipe #4: Cheesy Keto Quiche

Number of Servings: 8
Serving Size: 1/8 of the recipe

Prep Time: 15 minutes
Cook Time: 1 hour

Ingredients:
For the Crust:
- 2 large raw egg whites
- 1 cup almond flour
- 2/3 cup dry roasted macadamia nuts
- ¼ cup and 1 Tbsp. extra virgin olive oil
- ½ tsp. fine sea salt
- Nonstick cooking spray

For the Filling:
- 6 large eggs
- 1 cup 36 percent heavy cream
- ½ cup mild cheddar cheese
- Fine sea salt, to taste

Cooking Directions:

1. Set the oven to 350 degrees F to preheat. Lightly coat a 9-inch pie pan with nonstick cooking spray and set aside.

2. Prepare the crust a day ahead by combining all the ingredients in a bowl until the mixture turns into a dough. Transfer the dough onto the prepared pie pan and spread out until completely covered. If needed, transfer to the freezer and chill for 10 minutes to set.

3. Bake the crust for 25 minutes in the preheated oven until golden brown. Then, transfer to a cooling rack and let cool completely. Cover and refrigerate until ready to cook the quiche.

4. Prepare the quiche filling by combining the eggs, cheese, and heavy cream in a large bowl. Add a pinch of salt and mix well until smooth.

5. Pour the mixture into the prepared pie crust. Bake for 25 minutes, or until the quiche is just set. Insert a toothpick in the center of the quiche; if it comes out clean, it is ready.

6. Place the quiche on a cooling rack and allow to set for about 10 minutes. Slice and serve. Store in the refrigerator in an airtight container for up to 3 days.

Nutritional Facts per Serving:

Energy (calories)	166	kcal
Protein	2	g
Fat	17	g
Net Carbohydrates	2	g
Fiber	1	g
Sugars, total	0.94	g

Recipe #5: Blueberry Breakfast Scones

Number of Servings: 12

Serving Size: 1 scone

Prep Time: 10 minutes

Cook Time: 15 minutes

Ingredients:

- 3 large eggs, beaten
- 1 ½ cups almond flour
- ¾ cup fresh or frozen raspberries
- ½ cup stevia
- 2 tsp. pure vanilla extract
- 2 tsp. baking powder

Cooking Directions:

1. Set the oven to 375 degrees F to preheat. Line a baking sheet with baking paper and set aside.
2. In a large mixing bowl, beat the eggs together with the stevia, vanilla extract, baking powder, and then almond flour.
3. Fold the raspberries into the batter until evenly combined.
4. Scoop the batter onto the prepared baking sheet, about 3 tablespoons per mound. Ensure there is at least 2 inches of space between each scone.
5. Bake the scones for 15 minutes, or until golden brown.
6. Transfer the scones to a cooling rack and allow to set for 10 minutes. Then, transfer to an airtight container and store in a cool dry place for up to 3 days, or refrigerate for up to 5 days. Reheat before serving.

Nutritional Facts per Serving:

Energy (calories)	133	kcal
Protein	2	g
Fat	8	g
Net Carbohydrates	4	g
Fiber	2	g
Sugars, total	2	g

Recipe #6: Cinnamon Coconut Porridge

Number of Servings: 4
Serving Size: ½ cup

Prep Time: 5 minutes
Cook Time: 5 minutes

Ingredients:
- 2 cups water
- 1 cup 36 percent heavy cream
- ½ cup unsweetened dried shredded coconut
- 2 Tbsp. oat bran
- 2 Tbsp. flaxseed meal
- 1 Tbsp. butter
- 1 ½ tsp. stevia
- 1 tsp. cinnamon
- Fine sea salt, to taste

Cooking Directions:
1. Combine all the ingredients in a small pot and mix well until smooth.
2. Place the pot over medium low flame and bring to a slow boil. Once boiling, stir well and remove from the heat.
3. Divide into four equal servings and set aside for 10 minutes to thicken. Best served warm. Store in mason jars, seal tightly, and refrigerate for up to 2 days.

Nutritional Facts per Serving:

Energy (calories)	171	kcal
Protein	2	g

Fat	16	g
Net Carbohydrates	6	g
Fiber	2.5	g
Sugars, total	1.76	g

Recipe #7: Easy Scotch Eggs

Number of Servings: 6
Serving Size: 1 scotch egg

Prep Time: 15 minutes
Cook Time: 25 minutes

Ingredients:
- 6 hardboiled eggs, peeled
- 1 ½ cups breakfast sausage
- 1 ½ tsp. garlic powder
- 1/3 tsp. fine sea salt
- ½ tsp. freshly ground black pepper

Cooking Directions:
1. Set the oven to 400 degrees F to preheat.
2. Spread a large sheet of baking paper on a clean dry surface.
3. Place the breakfast sausage in a large bowl and add the salt, pepper, and garlic powder. Mix well with clean hands.
4. Divide the breakfast sausage mixture into 6 equal balls and arrange on the sheet of baking paper. Flatten the sausage balls out, then place a hardboiled egg on top. Wrap the egg with the sausage mixture.
5. Arrange the sausage-coated eggs on a dry baking sheet and bake in the preheated oven for 25 minutes.
6. Arrange the scotch eggs on a cooling rack and let set for 5 minutes. Store in an airtight container and refrigerate for up to 4 days. Reheat before serving.

Nutritional Facts per Serving:

Energy (calories)	258	kcal
Protein	17	g
Fat	21	g
Net Carbohydrates	1	g
Fiber	0	g
Sugars, total	1	g

Recipe #8: Easy Breakfast Tacos

Number of Servings: 2
Serving Size: ½ of the recipe

Prep Time: 10 minutes
Cook Time: 5 minutes

Ingredients:
- 2 low carb tortillas, about 36 grams each
- 4 large eggs
- ½ avocado, pitted, peeled and sliced into thin pieces
- 2 Tbsp. mayonnaise
- 1 Tbsp. butter
- 4 fresh cilantro sprigs
- Tabasco sauce, to taste
- Sea salt, to taste
- Freshly ground black pepper, to taste

Cooking Directions:
1. Whisk the eggs in a bowl until smooth. Set aside.
2. Place a nonstick skillet over medium flame and heat through. Once hot, add the butter and swirl to coat.
3. Add the egg and tilt until the eggs are spread out. Cook until done, then transfer to a bowl. Set aside.
4. Warm the tortillas over low flame, then place on a platter and spread the mayonnaise on one side of each tortilla.
5. Divide the egg between the two tortillas, then add the sliced avocado, and cilantro. Season with salt and pepper, then add the pepper sauce. Roll up the tortillas and serve.

6. To store, add lime juice all over the avocado first before placing in the tortilla. Wrap tightly in aluminum foil and store in the freezer for up to 1 day. Reheat in a toaster oven before serving.

Nutritional Facts per Serving:

Energy (calories)	289	kcal
Protein	7	g
Fat	27	g
Net Carbohydrates	6	g
Fiber	4	g
Sugars, total	0.67	g

Recipe #9: Bacon and Ricotta Breakfast Muffins

Number of Servings: 6
Serving Size: 2 muffins

Prep Time: 15 minutes
Cook Time: 30 minutes

Ingredients:

- 2 large eggs
- 1 lb. ricotta cheese
- 10 oz. baby spinach, rinsed and drained thoroughly
- 7 oz. bacon
- 2 oz. chopped toasted pine nuts
- 1 cup freshly grated Parmesan cheese
- ½ cup thick plain Greek yogurt
- Sea salt, to taste
- Freshly ground black pepper, to taste
- Nonstick cooking spray, as needed

Cooking Directions:

1. Set the oven to 350 degrees F to preheat. Lightly coat a 12 cup muffin tin with nonstick cooking spray and set aside.
2. Bring a saucepan of water to a boil, then add the spinach and blanch for 30 minutes, or until wilted. Drain well and set aside in a colander.
3. Meanwhile, dice the bacon and set aside.
4. Once the spinach is drained, finely chop then transfer to a large bowl. Add the ricotta cheese, pine nuts, Parmesan cheese, yogurt, eggs, and bacon. Mix very well until evenly combined.

5. Divide the mixture among the muffin cups, then bake for 30 minutes or until golden brown.

6. Place on a cooling rack and allow to cool slightly. Store in an airtight container and refrigerate for up to 3 days, or freeze for up to 3 weeks. Reheat in the microwave before serving.

Nutritional Facts per Serving:

Energy (calories)	440	kcal
Protein	27	g
Fat	29	g
Net Carbohydrates	22	g
Fiber	4	g
Sugars, total	3	g

Recipe #10: Keto Mini Waffles

Number of Servings: 8
Serving Size: 1 waffle

Prep Time: 15 minutes
Cook Time: 10 minutes

Ingredients:

- 2 large eggs
- ½ cup almond flour
- 4 Tbsp. full fat sour cream
- 2 Tbsp. melted grass-fed butter
- 4 tsp. arrowroot flour
- 2 tsp. cider vinegar
- 1 ½ tsp. stevia
- ¼ tsp. baking powder
- ¼ tsp. baking soda
- 1/8 tsp. xanthan gum
- 1/8 tsp. fine sea salt

Cooking Directions:

1. Combine the sour cream, egg, and vinegar with the melted butter in a bowl. Mix well.

2. Sift the dry ingredients into the sour cream and egg mixture. Then, stir gently until smooth.

3. Preheat a mini-waffle iron set on low. Once hot, cook the batter into 8 mini-waffles (or 4 regular-sized waffles) until firm.

4. Transfer to a tray and serve warm. May be stored in the freezer for up to 2 weeks. Reheat in the waffle iron before serving.

Nutritional Facts per Serving:

Energy (calories)	49	kcal
Protein	1	g
Fat	4	g
Net Carbohydrates	2	g
Fiber	0.1	g
Sugars, total	0.06	g

Recipe #11: Creamy Herbed Baked Eggs

Number of Servings: 4
Serving Size: ¼ of the recipe

Prep Time: 10 minutes
Cook Time: 20 minutes

Ingredients:

- 4 large eggs
- 60 grams 36 percent heavy cream
- 2 Tbsp. grass-fed butter, at room temperature
- 4 tsp. chopped fresh parsley
- 4 tsp. chopped fresh chives
- Sea salt, to taste
- Freshly ground black pepper, to taste

Cooking Directions:

1. Set the oven to 350 degrees F to preheat. Use 1 tablespoon of butter to coat four 1-cup ovenproof ramekins.
2. Crack an egg into each ramekin, then divide the heavy cream among them. Top with the fresh parsley and chives. Season with salt and pepper.
3. Arrange the ramekins on a baking sheet and bake for 20 minutes, or until the eggs are set.
4. Transfer to a cooling rack and let stand for 5 minutes before serving. To store, cover with aluminum foil and refrigerate for up to 2 days. Reheat in the microwave before serving.

Nutritional Facts per Serving:

Energy (calories)	158	kcal
Protein	3	g
Fat	16	g
Net Carbohydrates	1	g
Fiber	0.1	g
Sugars, total	0.5	g

Recipe #12: Keto Bread

Number of Servings: 6
Serving Size: 1/6 of the recipe

Prep Time: 1 hour and 30 minutes
Cook Time: 1 hour

Ingredients:

- 3 large eggs
- 1/3 cup full fat cream cheese, at room temperature
- 4 ½ Tbsp. flaxseed meal
- 1 ½ Tbsp. and 1 ½ tsp. melted coconut oil
- 6 tsp. psyllium powder
- 3 tsp. coconut flour
- 3 tsp. cider vinegar
- 3 tsp. warm water
- 2 ¼ tsp. stevia
- 1/3 tsp. baking soda
- 1/3 tsp. baking powder
- 1/6 tsp. xanthan gum
- 1/6 tsp. fine sea salt

Cooking Directions:

1. Set the oven to 350 degrees F to preheat. Cover a baking sheet with baking paper and set aside.
2. Mix together all the dry ingredients in a bowl very well, then set aside.
3. In a separate bowl, whisk together all the wet ingredients. Then, gradually mix in the dry ingredients until smooth.
4. Divide the mixture into six equal sized rolls then arrange on the prepared baking sheet. Cover with a clean kitchen towel and let rise for about 30 minutes to an hour.

5. Once the rolls have risen to double their size, bake the rolls for 40 minutes. Insert a toothpick in the center of one roll; if it comes out clean, it is ready.

6. Transfer the rolls on a cooling rack and allow to cool slightly. Best served right away. May be stored for up to 3 days in an airtight container away from direct sunlight.

Nutritional Facts per Serving:

Energy (calories)	106	kcal
Protein	4	g
Fat	9	g
Net Carbohydrates	4	g
Fiber	2	g
Sugars, total	1	g

Chapter 4 – Keto Meal Prep Lunch Recipes

Recipe #1: Savory Beef Balls with Asian Style Dip

Number of Servings: 5
Serving Size: 6 meatballs

Prep Time: 15 minutes
Cook Time: 15 minutes

Ingredients:
- 1 lb. organic ground beef
- 1 large egg
- 1 small red onion, peeled and minced
- 2 garlic cloves, peeled and minced
- ½ tsp. sea salt
- Freshly ground black pepper, to taste

For the Sauce:
- 1 garlic clove, peeled and minced
- ¼ cup light soy sauce
- 2 Tbsp. rice wine vinegar
- 1 Tbsp. freshly grated ginger
- 1 Tbsp. chopped green onion
- Liquid stevia, to taste
- Nonstick cooking spray, as needed

Cooking Directions:

1. Set the oven to 425 degrees F to preheat. Lightly coat a baking sheet with nonstick cooking spray and set aside.

2. Place the ground beef in a large mixing bowl and add the egg, onion, salt, garlic, and a generous pinch of black pepper. Mix everything well with clean hands.

3. Make about 40 1-inch sized balls from the meat mixture and arrange them on the prepared baking sheet.

4. Bake the meatballs in the preheated oven for about 12 minutes, or until browned all over but still moist.

5. While the meatballs are cooking, combine all the sauce ingredients in a dipping bowl and stir well.

6. Once the meatballs are cooked, transfer them to an airtight container and allow to cool slightly before sealing. Store the dipping sauce in a separate airtight container.

7. Refrigerate the meatballs and sauce for up to 3 days, or freeze for up to 3 weeks. Reheat before serving.

Nutritional Facts per Serving:

Energy (calories)	238	kcal
Protein	24	g
Fat	14	g
Net Carbohydrates	3	g
Fiber	0.4	g
Sugars, total	0.8	g

Recipe #2: Chicken Curry with Oil-Roasted Peanuts

Number of Servings: 3
Serving Size: 1/3 of the recipe

Prep Time: 15 minutes
Cook Time: 20 minutes

Ingredients:

- 1 garlic clove, peeled and minced
- 7.5 oz. full fat unsweetened coconut milk
- ½ lb. chicken breast, sliced into thin strips
- ¼ cup diced yellow onion
- ¼ cup water
- ¼ cup oil roasted peanuts
- 2 Tbsp. chopped fresh cilantro
- 1 ½ Tbsp. melted coconut oil
- 1 ½ Tbsp. melted palm oil
- ½ Tbsp. curry powder
- 1 tsp. minced fresh ginger
- Sea salt, to taste
- Red pepper flakes, to taste

Cooking Directions:

1. Place a saucepan over medium flame and add the coconut and palm oil. Swirl to combine.
2. Stir in the onion and curry powder then sauté until the onions are tender.
3. Stir in the sliced chicken and sauté until the chicken is cooked through. Then, add the ginger and garlic and sauté until fragrant.
4. Add the water and coconut milk then bring to a boil.

5. Once boiling, reduce to simmer and stir in the peanuts. Continue to simmer until the curry is thickened and the chicken is completely cooked.

6. Remove the curry from heat and stir in the cilantro. Season to taste with salt and red pepper flakes.

7. Divide between two airtight containers and allow to cool slightly. Cover and refrigerate for up to 3 days. Reheat before serving.

Nutritional Facts per Serving:

Energy (calories)	586	kcal
Protein	18	g
Fat	56	g
Net Carbohydrates	6	g
Fiber	2	g
Sugars, total	3	g

Recipe #3: Baked Parmesan Chicken Nuggets in Mozzarella Marinara Sauce

Number of Servings: 6
Serving Size: 4 nuggets

Prep Time: 20 minutes
Cook Time: 45 minutes

Ingredients:

- 1 lb. finely minced chicken breast
- 3 oz. fresh mozzarella cheese
- 1 cup almond flour
- 1 cup marinara sauce, no sugar added
- ½ cup full cream milk
- ½ cup freshly grated Parmesan cheese
- 1 tsp. fine sea salt
- ½ tsp. dried oregano
- Freshly ground black pepper, to taste
- Nonstick cooking spray, as needed

Cooking Directions:

1. Set the oven to 350 degrees F to preheat. Lightly coat a large baking dish and set aside.

2. In a large mixing bowl, combine half the almond flour with the milk, parmesan cheese, salt, and a pinch of black pepper. Mix everything well.

3. Add the minced chicken into the almond flour mixture and mix well until evenly combined.

4. Divide the mixture into 24 equal balls then dredge the balls in the reserved almond flour.

5. Arrange the balls on the prepared baking dish, then bake for 10 minutes.

6. After 10 minutes, turn over the balls and bake for an additional 10 minutes.

7. Once the balls are baked, pour the marinara sauce over them then dot with pieces of mozzarella cheese.

8. Bake for an additional 12 to 15 minutes, or until the cheese is melted.

9. Remove from the oven and top with dried oregano.

10. Allow to cool slightly, then cover and refrigerate for up to 3 days. Reheat before serving.

Nutritional Facts per Serving:

Energy (calories)	282	kcal
Protein	33	g
Fat	12	g
Net Carbohydrates	11	g
Fiber	3	g
Sugars, total	4	g

Recipe #4: Zucchini Beef Lasagna

Number of Servings: 10
Serving Size: 1/10 of the recipe

Prep Time: 20 minutes
Cook Time: 1 hour

Ingredients:
- 2 large zucchinis
- 1 large yellow onion, chopped
- 2 garlic cloves, peeled and minced
- 1 lb. 75 percent lean ground beef
- 2 cups no sugar organic pasta sauce
- 1 cup ricotta cheese
- ½ cup shredded Parmesan cheese
- 8 Tbsp. shredded mozzarella cheese
- 2 Tbsp. chopped fresh oregano
- 2 Tbsp. olive oil
- 1 Tbsp. chopped fresh basil
- ¼ tsp. fine sea salt
- ¼ tsp. freshly ground black pepper

Cooking Directions:
1. Set the oven to 375 degrees F to preheat.
2. Place a saucepan over medium high flame and heat through. Once hot, add the olive oil and swirl to coat.
3. Sauté the onion in the saucepan until tender, then stir in the garlic and sauté until fragrant.

4. Add the ground beef to the saucepan and stir, breaking up, until browned all over.

5. Stir in the pasta sauce then bring to a simmer. Once simmering, reduce to low flame and stir in the basil, oregano, and salt. Mix well then set aside.

6. Halve the zucchinis lengthwise, then slice into extra thin strips, about 1/8 inch thick.

7. Arrange 6 zucchini slices on the bottom of the baking dish, then add a quarter of the meat sauce on top. Add ¼ cup of the ricotta cheese with 2 tablespoons or mozzarella cheese. Repeat, ensuring the zucchini slices crisscross.

8. Once the lasagna is assembled, top with Parmesan cheese and black pepper. Bake in the oven for 1 hour, or until the top is browned and bubbling.

9. Carefully remove the lasagna from the oven and place on the kitchen counter. Allow to set for about 15 minutes, then slice into 10 equal servings.

10. Allow to cool slightly, then cover and refrigerate for up to 4 days. Reheat before serving.

Nutritional Facts per Serving:

Energy (calories)	366	kcal
Protein	46	g
Fat	15	g
Net Carbohydrates	12	g
Fiber	4	g
Sugars, total	6	g

Recipe #5: Chicken Bell Pepper Kebabs

Number of Servings: 4
Serving Size: 2 kebabs

Prep Time: 15 minutes
Cook Time: 12 minutes

Ingredients:

- 2 lbs. boneless and skinless chicken breasts
- 3 garlic cloves, peeled and crushed
- 1 large red bell pepper, stemmed, seeded, and sliced into bite-sized chunks
- 1 large green bell pepper, stemmed, seeded, and sliced into bite-sized chunks
- ¾ cup olive oil
- 2 ½ Tbsp. freshly squeezed lemon juice
- 1 Tbsp. chopped fresh parsley
- 2 ½ tsp. freshly grated lemon zest
- Sea salt, to taste
- Freshly ground black pepper, to taste

Cooking Directions:

1. If using wooden skewers, then soak in ice water.
2. Rinse the chicken breasts thoroughly then blot dry with paper towels and set aside.
3. Chop the chicken breasts into bite-sized chunks then set aside.
4. Combine ¼ cup of the olive oil with the crushed garlic, and lemon zest. Mix well, then stir in the parsley with a pinch of salt and pepper. Mix well.
5. Place the chicken cubes into the mixture and toss several times to coat. Once mixed, cover and refrigerate for up to 12 hours to marinate.

6. Once ready to cook, combine the remaining olive oil with the lemon juice then season to taste with salt and pepper.

7. Set the broiler or grill to medium to preheat.

8. Skewer the chicken and bell peppers, alternating the three. Then, coat the kebabs in the lemon and olive oil mixture.

9. Broil the skewered chicken and pepper for 10 minutes, turning and basting occasionally. Once the chicken is cooked and the bell peppers are browned, transfer to a platter.

10. Allow the chicken and bell pepper kebabs to cool slightly, then store in an airtight container and refrigerate for up to 3 days. Reheat before serving.

Nutritional Facts per Serving:

Energy (calories)	287	kcal
Protein	52	g
Fat	20	g
Net Carbohydrates	4	g
Fiber	0.5	g
Sugars, total	1.4	g

Recipe #6: Easy Grilled Shrimp with Avocado, Tomato and Onion Salad

Number of Servings: 6
Serving Size: 1/6 of the recipe

Prep Time: 20 minutes
Cook Time: 5 minutes

Ingredients:
- 2 avocados, pitted, peeled and cubed
- 2 lb. shrimp, peeled and deveined
- ½ cup chopped tomato
- ½ cup chopped bell pepper
- ½ cup chopped onion
- 4 Tbsp. olive oil
- 2 tsp. freshly squeezed lime juice
- 1 tsp. garlic powder
- 1 tsp. fine sea salt
- ¼ tsp. freshly ground black pepper

Cooking Directions:
1. Place a grill over medium high flame and heat through.
2. Meanwhile, combine the garlic powder, half the salt and pepper, and olive oil in a large bowl. Add the shrimp and toss well to coat. Set aside.
3. In a salad bowl, combine the bell pepper, tomato, onion, avocado, and lime juice. Season with the remaining salt and toss gently to coat. Cover and refrigerate until ready to serve.

4. Cook the shrimp in the hot grill for 3 minutes per side, or until cooked through.

5. Divide the shrimp into individual servings, followed by the salad. Cover and refrigerate for up to 3 days. Reheat the shrimp before serving.

Nutritional Facts per Serving:

Energy (calories)	409	kcal
Protein	36	g
Fat	25	g
Net Carbohydrates	11	g
Fiber	5	g
Sugars, total	5	g

Recipe #7: Mediterranean Style Tuna Salad

Number of Servings: 6
Serving Size: ½ cup

Prep Time: 15 minutes

Ingredients:
- 300 grams endives, leaves separated
- 15 oz. solid white albacore tuna packed in oil, drained
- 1 ½ cups crumbled feta cheese
- ¾ cup extra virgin olive oil
- ¾ cup diced roasted red peppers
- 1/3 cup quartered green olives
- 1/3 cup chopped fresh parsley
- 1 ½ Tbsp. freshly squeezed lemon juice
- 1 ½ Tbsp. drained capers
- Red pepper flakes, to taste
- Fine sea salt, to taste
- Freshly ground black pepper, to taste

Cooking Directions:
1. Place the tuna in a bowl and crumble. Fold in the feta cheese, roasted red peppers, green olives, capers, parsley, lemon juice, and olive oil. Mix well.
2. Season the tuna mixture to taste with salt, pepper, and red pepper flakes then mix well to combine.
3. Divide the salad into six equal portions in airtight containers then add the endive leaves. Cover and refrigerate for up to 3 days. Serve chilled.

Nutritional Facts per Serving:

Energy (calories)	352	kcal
Protein	25	g
Fat	26	g
Net Carbohydrates	5	g
Fiber	2	g
Sugars, total	3	g

Recipe #8: Creamy Cauli Mac 'n' Cheese

Number of Servings: 4
Serving Size: ¼ of the recipe

Prep Time: 10 minutes
Cook Time: 30 minutes

Ingredients:
- 1 small cauliflower head, chopped into small florets
- ½ cup heavy cream
- ½ cup shredded Cheddar cheese
- ¼ cup shredded mozzarella cheese
- ¼ cup shredded Parmesan cheese
- ¼ cup cubed cream cheese
- ½ tsp. fine sea salt
- ¼ tsp. minced garlic
- 1/8 tsp. freshly ground black pepper
- Nonstick cooking spray, as needed

Cooking Directions:
1. Set the oven to 400 degrees F to preheat.
2. Fill a small pot with water, cover and place over high flame. Bring to a boil, then add ¼ teaspoon of salt.
3. Add the cauliflower florets to the boiling water, then boil for about 3 minutes. Drain then place on a platter lined with paper towels and set aside.
4. Place a skillet over medium flame and add the heavy cream. Bring to a simmer, then stir in the cream cheese until smooth.
5. Stir in the Cheddar cheese, garlic, and mozzarella cheese, then stir until melted.

6. Turn off the heat and mix in the cauliflower. Stir until the cauliflower is completely coated. Season with salt and pepper.

7. Lightly coat a small baking dish with nonstick cooking spray. Add the cauliflower and cheese mixture, then sprinkle the Parmesan cheese on top.

8. Bake the mac and cheese for 15 minutes, or until the top is golden brown.

9. Place on a cooling rack and allow to cool slightly. Slice into four equal servings, then cover and refrigerate for up to 3 days. Reheat before serving.

Nutritional Facts per Serving:

Energy (calories)	198	kcal
Protein	10	g
Fat	17	g
Net Carbohydrates	3	g
Fiber	0.9	g
Sugars, total	2	g

Recipe #9: Balsamic Herbed Pork Tenderloin

Number of Servings: 2
Serving Size: ½ of the recipe

Prep Time: 15 minutes
Cook Time: 20 minutes

Ingredients:

- ¾ lb. pork tenderloin, sliced into 1 ½ inch thick medallions
- 1 garlic clove, peeled and minced
- 1 small shallot, minced
- 3 Tbsp. butter
- 2 Tbsp. balsamic vinegar
- 1 ½ Tbsp. olive oil
- ¾ tsp. soy sauce
- 3 fresh rosemary sprigs
- 3 fresh thyme sprigs
- Sea salt, to taste
- Freshly ground black pepper, to taste

Cooking Directions:

1. Set the oven to 475 degrees F to preheat.
2. Blot the pork medallions dry with paper towels then season with salt and pepper.
3. Place an ovenproof skillet over medium high flame and heat through. Once hot, add the olive oil and ¾ tablespoon of butter then swirl to coat.
4. Add the garlic and shallot then sauté until fragrant. Add the pork medallions and sear for 2 minutes per side.

5. Stir in the balsamic vinegar, soy sauce, thyme, rosemary, and remaining butter. Stir well to combine, then spoon the mixture over the pork.

6. Simmer for 2 minutes, then bake for 5 minutes.

7. After 5 minutes, turn over the pork medallions and cook for an added 5 minutes, or until the internal temperature of the pork is 150 degrees F.

8. Transfer the pork to a platter and let rest for 3 minutes. Then, divide into individual servings and spoon the sauce on top. Cover and refrigerate for up to 3 days.

Nutritional Facts per Serving:

Energy (calories)	508	kcal
Protein	45	g
Fat	34	g
Net Carbohydrates	4	g
Fiber	0.1	g
Sugars, total	3	g

Recipe #10: Keto Squash-getti with Herbed Meatballs

Number of Servings: 6
Serving Size: 1/6 of the recipe

Prep Time: 20 minutes
Cook Time: 30 minutes

Ingredients:

- 1 extra large or 2 medium spaghetti squash
- ¾ cup chopped fresh parsley
- 4 ½ Tbsp. water
- 3 Tbsp. olive oil

For the Herbed Meatballs

- 2 garlic cloves, peeled and minced
- ¾ lb. lean ground beef, 80 percent
- ¾ lb. ground pork
- 1 ½ cup organic pasta sauce, no sugar added
- ¾ cup shredded Parmesan cheese
- 3 Tbsp. chopped fresh oregano
- 3 Tbsp. chopped fresh basil
- ¾ tsp. onion powder
- 1/3 tsp. fine sea salt
- 1/3 tsp. freshly ground black pepper

Cooking Directions:

1. Halve the spaghetti squash lengthwise. Scoop out and discard the seeds, then place on a microwaveable dish, cut side face down. Microwave for 12 minutes on high.
2. Carefully scoop out the squash mixture from the shells using a large fork and transfer to a bowl.

3. Place a skillet over medium high flame and heat through. Add 1 ½ tablespoons of olive oil and swirl to coat.

4. Add the squash and stir well until browned. Transfer to a bowl and fold in 1/3 cup of parsley. Set aside.

5. Pour the remaining parsley in a large bowl, then mix in the pork, beef, oregano, basil, garlic, onion powder, 1/3 cup of the Parmesan cheese, and salt and pepper. Mix well with clean hands.

6. Divide the mixture into 18 equal sized balls, then arrange on a platter.

7. Place a heavy duty skillet over medium high flame and heat through. Once hot, add the remaining olive oil and swirl to coat.

8. Cook the meatballs, in batches, if needed, for 2 minutes per side, or until cooked through.

9. Once all the meatballs are cooked, return them all to the skillet and add the pasta sauce. Bring to a simmer, then stir and reduce to low flame. Simmer for 15 minutes.

10. Divide the spaghetti squash into individual servings then divide the meatballs as well. Sprinkle with the remaining Parmesan cheese, then let cool slightly. Cover and refrigerate for up to 3 days. Reheat before serving.

Nutritional Facts per Serving:

Energy (calories)	460	kcal
Protein	43	g
Fat	28	g
Net Carbohydrates	11	g
Fiber	1	g
Sugars, total	9	g

Recipe #11: Sardine and Garden Salad

Number of Servings: 3
Serving Size: 1/3 of the recipe

Prep Time: 15 minutes

Ingredients:

- 1 cucumber, quartered and diced
- 2 large tomatoes, diced
- 1 small red onion, peeled and minced
- 2 sardine fillets packed in oil, drained and chopped
- 2 sardine fillets packed in oil, drained
- 2 cups arugula leaves, chopped
- ¼ cup chopped fresh flat leaf parsley

For the dressing:

- 2 Tbsp. extra virgin olive oil
- ½ Tbsp. freshly squeezed lemon juice
- Sea salt, to taste
- Freshly ground black pepper, to taste

Cooking Directions:

1. Combine the ingredients for the dressing in a bowl and set aside.
2. Toss together the chopped sardines, vegetables, and herbs in a bowl. Mix well, then divide into individual servings.
3. Divide the whole sardine fillets among the servings.
4. Drizzle the dressing over the salads, then cover and refrigerate for up to 3 days.

Nutritional Facts per Serving:

Energy (calories)	150	kcal
Protein	6	g
Fat	11	g
Net Carbohydrates	8	g
Fiber	2	g
Sugars, total	5	g

Recipe #12: Herbed Parmesan Chicken Fingers

Number of Servings: 6
Serving Size: 4 chicken fingers

Prep Time: 15 minutes
Cook Time: 30 minutes

Ingredients:

- 2 lbs. boneless and skinless chicken breast
- 4 garlic cloves, peeled and chopped
- 4 oz. butter
- 1 cup freshly grated Parmesan cheese
- 2 Tbsp. chopped fresh thyme
- 1 tsp. chili pepper flakes
- Sea salt, to taste
- Freshly ground black pepper, to taste
- Nonstick cooking spray

Cooking Directions:

1. Set the oven to 350 degrees F to preheat. Lightly coat a baking sheet with nonstick cooking spray and set aside.

2. Place a saucepan over medium flame and heat through. Add the butter and swirl to melt.

3. Stir the garlic into the saucepan and sauté until fragrant. Remove from heat and set aside for 15 minutes.

4. Combine the thyme, Parmesan cheese, chili pepper, and a pinch of salt and pepper. Stir well to combine then set aside.

5. Rinse the chicken breast thoroughly then blot dry with paper towels. Slice into 24 fingers, then coat in the garlic butter mixture.

6. Dredge the chicken fingers in the cheesy mixture then arrange on the prepared baking sheet.

7. Bake for 25 to 30 minutes, or until the chicken fingers are golden brown and cooked through.

8. Transfer the chicken fingers to a cooling rack and allow to cool completely. Store in an airtight container and refrigerate for up to 3 days. Reheat before serving.

Nutritional Facts per Serving:

Energy (calories)	370	kcal
Protein	40	g
Fat	20	g
Net Carbohydrates	6	g
Fiber	0.2	g
Sugars, total	0.2	g

Recipe #13: Ham, Onion and Green Bean Salad

Number of Servings: 3
Serving Size: 1/3 of the recipe

Prep Time: 15 minutes

Ingredients:

- ½ lb. trimmed green beans, steamed
- 1 small white onion, peeled and minced
- 1 roasted red bell pepper, drained and diced
- 1 oz. Spanish ham, chopped
- 1 small hardboiled egg, chopped
- 2 ½ Tbsp. fresh flat leaf parsley
- 2 Tbsp. extra virgin olive oil
- 1 ½ Tbsp. red wine vinegar
- Sea salt, to taste
- Freshly ground black pepper, to taste

Cooking Directions:

1. Rinse and drain the steamed green beans. Blot dry with paper towels and set aside.
2. Combine the olive oil, vinegar, and a dash of salt and pepper. Mix well.
3. Divide the green beans into individual servings, followed by the minced onion, ham, peppers, egg, and parsley. Add the dressing.
4. Cover and refrigerate for up to 2 days. Reheat before serving, if desired.

Nutritional Facts per Serving:

Energy (calories)   102   kcal

Protein	4	g
Fat	8	g
Net Carbohydrates	5	g
Fiber	2	g
Sugars, total	2	g

Recipe #14: Cheesy Avocado Beef Patties

Number of Servings: 2
Serving Size: 1 patty

Prep Time: 15 minutes
Cook Time: 10 minutes

Ingredients:
- ½ lb. 85 percent lean ground beef
- 1 small avocado, pitted and peeled
- 2 slices yellow cheddar cheese
- Sea salt, to taste
- Freshly ground black pepper, to taste

Cooking Directions:
1. Preheat the broiler or grill to high.
2. Divide the ground beef into two equal sized patties. Season with salt and pepper.
3. Grill or broil the beef patties for about 5 minutes per side, or until cooked through.
4. Transfer the patties to a platter and add the cheese. To store, wrap in aluminum foil and refrigerate for up to 3 days.
5. Right before serving, reheat the burger patty in a microwave oven. Slice the avocado into thin strips and place on top of the patty. Serve warm, preferably with a light, low carb salad.

Nutritional Facts per Serving:
Energy (calories)   568   kcal

Protein	38	g
Fat	43	g
Net Carbohydrates	9	g
Fiber	7	g
Sugars, total	0.74	g

Recipe #15: Cheesy Sausage, Mushroom and Spaghetti Squash Casserole

Number of Servings: 10
Serving Size: 1/10 of the recipe

Prep Time: 30 minutes
Cook Time: 1 ½ hours

Ingredients:

- 1 large spaghetti squash
- 1 large onion, peeled and minced
- ½ lb. lean organic ground beef, 80 percent
- ½ lb. Italian sausage
- ½ lb. chicken or turkey sausage
- ½ lb. sliced mushrooms
- 18 oz. diced tomatoes
- 8 oz. freshly grated Parmesan cheese
- 6 oz. organic tomato paste
- 4 oz. mozzarella cheese
- 4 oz. ricotta cheese
- ½ cup butter
- ½ cup red wine
- ½ tsp. sea salt
- ½ tsp. freshly ground black pepper

Cooking Directions:

1. Set the oven to 350 degrees F to preheat.
2. Pierce the spaghetti squash all over with a sharp then place in the microwave and microwave on high for about 20 minutes. set aside to cool.

3. Melt the butter in a skillet over medium high flame. Sauté the ground beef and sausages until cooked through and crumbled.

4. Add the red wine and simmer until liquid is reduced. Then, stir in the onion and garlic. Sauté until tender.

5. Add the mushrooms and sauté until tender. Stir in the diced tomatoes, tomato paste, and seasonings. Sauté until combined.

6. Halve the spaghetti squash and scrape out the flesh. Set aside.

7. Spread half the spaghetti squash in a baking dish then add 2 ounces each of the mozzarella and ricotta, followed by 4 ounces of the Parmesan.

8. Spoon some tomato sauce on top, then add the remaining spaghetti squash. Add the remaining cheeses, then cover the dish.

9. Bake for 20 minutes, then uncover and bake for an additional 20 minutes.

10. Set the oven to broil and broil the casserole for 3 minutes, or until the top is browned and crisp.

11. Place on a cooling rack and let set for 15 minutes. Slice into 10 equal servings, then cover and refrigerate for up to 5 days. Reheat before serving.

Nutritional Facts per Serving:

Energy (calories)	402	kcal
Protein	31	g
Fat	24	g
Net Carbohydrates	15	g
Fiber	2	g
Sugars, total	2	g

Chapter 5 – Keto Meal Prep Dinner Recipes

Recipe #1: Deviled Eggs with Chopped Bacon

Number of Servings: 6
Serving Size: 3 stuffed halved eggs

Prep Time: 5 minutes
Cook Time: 15 minutes

Ingredients:

- 9 large eggs
- 6 bacon slices, chopped
- 2 ¼ Tbsp. mayonnaise
- 1 ½ Tbsp. mustard
- ¾ tsp. paprika
- 1/6 tsp. fine sea salt
- 1/6 tsp. freshly ground black pepper

Cooking Directions:

1. Place the eggs in a pot and add enough water to cover them by about an inch. Cover and place over high flame. Bring to a boil.

2. Once boiling, reduce to a simmer, then simmer for 3 minutes. Turn off the heat and keep the eggs in the hot water.

3. Meanwhile, place a large skillet over medium high flame and heat through. Once hot, add the bacon and cook until crisp.

4. Transfer the bacon to a plate lined with paper towels and allow to drain.

5. Take the eggs out of the water and transfer to a basin of cold water. Once cool to the touch, carefully peel them.

6. Halve the hardboiled eggs carefully then scoop out the yolks and place in a bowl. Arrange the halves, cut side facing up, on a platter and set aside.

7. Mash the yolks together with the mustard, mayonnaise, salt, and pepper. Add 1/3 teaspoon of the paprika and mix well.

8. Dice the drained crispy bacon. Pour 1/3 cup of the chopped bacon into the bowl of yolk mixture and stir well.

9. Spoon the yolk mixture among the halved egg whites, then divide the reserved bacon among them.

10. Sprinkle with paprika and serve. Store the extra devilled eggs in an airtight container and refrigerate for up to 3 days.

Nutritional Facts per Serving:

Energy (calories)	283	kcal
Protein	20	g
Fat	21	g
Net Carbohydrates	3	g
Fiber	0.5	g
Sugars, total	2	g

Recipe #2: Keto Caesar Salad

Number of Servings: 6
Serving Size: 2 cups

Prep Time: 15 minutes

Ingredients:

- 12 cups chopped romaine lettuce
- 1/3 cup extra virgin olive oil
- 1/3 cup freshly grated Parmesan cheese
- 3 Tbsp. freshly squeezed lemon juice
- 1 ½ Tbsp. mayonnaise
- 1/3 tsp. anchovy paste
- 1/3 tsp. garlic powder
- Freshly ground black pepper, to taste

Cooking Directions:

1. Combine the lemon juice, olive oil, anchovy paste, garlic powder, and mayonnaise in an airtight container. Whisk well until thoroughly combined. Divide into 6 equal servings in small airtight containers and refrigerate for up to 3 days.

2. In a large bowl, toss together the lettuce and Parmesan cheese. Season lightly with black pepper and toss again to coat. Divide into 6 airtight containers then cover and refrigerate for up to 3 days.

3. Right before serving, add the dressing to the salad. Toss to coat then serve right away.

Nutritional Facts per Serving:

Energy (calories)   93   kcal

Protein	3	g
Fat	7	g
Net Carbohydrates	6	g
Fiber	2	g
Sugars, total	1	g

Recipe #3: Fried Cheesy Avocado Wedges

Number of Servings: 4
Serving Size: ¼ of the recipe

Prep Time: 5 minutes
Cook Time: 10 minutes

Ingredients:
- 2 small eggs
- 1 large avocado
- 1/3 cup ground pork rinds
- 1/3 cup shredded Parmesan cheese
- 1 ½ Tbsp. heavy cream
- 1/3 tsp. garlic powder
- 1/3 tsp. onion powder
- 1/3 tsp. fine sea salt
- 1/3 tsp. freshly ground black pepper
- Sunflower oil, as needed

Cooking Directions:

1. Place a heavy duty skillet over medium flame and add approximately 1 ½ inches of oil. Heat the oil to 375 degrees F.
2. Meanwhile, whisk the eggs in a small bowl then mix in until smooth.
3. Halve the avocado carefully then discard the stone. Scoop out the flesh using a spoon then slice into ½ inch thick wedges.
4. Season the avocado wedges with salt and pepper then set aside.
5. On a plate, combine the pork rinds, onion and garlic powders, and Parmesan cheese. Mix well.

6. Dip the avocado wedges in the egg mixture, then drain and dredge in the pork rind and Parmesan cheese mixture until completely covered.

7. Add the coated wedges in the hot oil and cook for 1 minute per side, or until golden brown.

8. Transfer the wedges to a platter lined with paper towels and let drain. Allow to cool slightly, then transfer to an airtight container and refrigerate for up to 2 days. Reheat before serving in hot oil, if desired.

Nutritional Facts per Serving:

Energy (calories)	179	kcal
Protein	8	g
Fat	14	g
Net Carbohydrates	6	g
Fiber	3	g
Sugars, total	0.5	g

Recipe #4: Simple Beef Chili

Number of Servings: 3
Serving Size: ½ cup

Prep Time: 15 minutes
Cook Time: 1 hour

Ingredients:
- 1 small yellow onion, peeled and diced
- 1 lb. 85 percent ground beef
- 2 cups organic beef broth
- ¼ cup extra virgin olive oil
- 2 Tbsp. flaxseed meal
- 1 Tbsp. chili powder
- 1 tsp. dried oregano
- ½ tsp. cumin seeds
- ¼ tsp. garlic powder
- Sea salt, to taste
- Freshly ground black pepper, to taste

Cooking Directions:
1. Place a heavy duty pot over high flame and heat through. Once hot, add the beef and onion and sauté until the beef is browned.
2. Stir in the chili powder, oregano, cumin seeds, and garlic powder then sauté until combined.
3. Pour in the beef broth, flaxseed meal, and olive oil. Stir to combine, then bring to a boil.

4. Once boiling, reduce to medium high flame and simmer, partially covered, for 1 hour or until the chili is thickened.

5. Remove from heat and cover. Allow to cool, then transfer to airtight containers and refrigerate for up to 3 days. Reheat and season to taste with salt and pepper before serving.

Nutritional Facts per Serving:

Energy (calories)	567	kcal
Protein	41	g
Fat	36	g
Net Carbohydrates	18	g
Fiber	3	g
Sugars, total	0.3	g

Recipe #5: Low Carb Hearty Pot Roast

Number of Servings: 3
Serving Size: 1/3 of the recipe

Prep Time: 35 minutes
Cook Time: 5 hours

Ingredients:

- 2 ½ lb. bottom round rump roast
- 1 small onion, peeled and quartered
- 1 large garlic clove, peeled
- 1 fresh thyme sprig
- 1 turnip, peeled and chopped
- 1 ½ cups beef stock
- 1 cup halved radishes
- 2 Tbsp. heavy cream
- 1 ½ Tbsp. olive oil
- Sea salt, to taste
- Freshly ground black pepper, to taste

Cooking Directions:

1. Set the oven to 475 degrees F.
2. Season the pork all over with salt and pepper.
3. Place a Dutch oven over high flame and add the olive oil. Swirl to coat, then brown the roast all over and set aside.
4. Sauté the onion in the same pot until browned then transfer to the bowl with the pot roast.
5. Add the beef stock, garlic, and thyme, then mix well. Return the roast and onion, then add the radishes and turnips.

6. Place the pot, uncovered, in the oven and set it to 400 degrees F. Cook for 4 to 5 hours, or until the internal temperature of the pot roast is 130 degrees F.

7. Take the roast out of the pot and let cool. Then, transfer the vegetables and roast to a bowl.

8. Place a saucepan over medium flame and add the liquid from the Dutch oven. Stir in the heavy cream then bring to a boil. Then, reduce to a simmer.

9. Slice the pot roast thinly, then divide into individual servings. Divide the vegetables and sauce as well, then let cool slightly. Cover and refrigerate for up to 3 days.

Nutritional Facts per Serving:

Energy (calories)	521	kcal
Protein	69	g
Fat	25	g
Net Carbohydrates	6	g
Fiber	4	g
Sugars, total	4	g

Recipe #6: Miso Beef and Tender Zucchini

Number of Servings: 2
Serving Size: ½ of the recipe

Prep Time: 15 minutes
Cook Time: 15 minutes

Ingredients:
- ½ lb. flank steak
- ½ lb. zucchini, julienned
- 3 oz. butter, at room temperature
- 2 Tbsp. water
- ¼ Tbsp. toasted sesame oil
- 2 tsp. white miso paste
- Sea salt, to taste
- Freshly ground black pepper, to taste

Cooking Directions:
1. Preheat the grill to high.
2. In a bowl, stir together the miso paste and butter until thoroughly combined. Cover then set aside.
3. Blot the flank steak dry with paper towels then season all over with salt and pepper.
4. Grill the flank steak until the internal temperature is at least 160 degrees F, or the beef is cooked through.
5. Transfer the beef to a sheet of aluminum foil and let rest for about 10 minutes.
6. Put the julienned zucchini in a bowl and add 2 tablespoons of water. Cover and steam for 2 minutes or until the zucchini is slightly tender.
7. Drain the zucchini then add the sesame oil. Toss to coat.

8. Slice the beef across the grain very thinly then divide into two portions. Place in an airtight container.

9. Divide the zucchini and add to the side. Spoon the butter mixture on top, then cover and refrigerate for up to 3 days. Reheat in the microwave before serving.

Nutritional Facts per Serving:

Energy (calories)	511	kcal
Protein	28	g
Fat	43	g
Net Carbohydrates	5	g
Fiber	2	g
Sugars, total	0.3	g

Recipe #7: Roasted Garlic Butter Cod with Bok Choy

Number of Servings: 3
Serving Size: 1 cod fillet

Prep Time: 5 minutes
Cook Time: 20 minutes

Ingredients:
- 3 cod fillets, 8 oz. each
- ¾ lb. baby bok choy, halved
- 1/3 cup thinly sliced butter
- 1 ½ Tbsp. minced garlic
- Sea salt, to taste
- Freshly ground black pepper, to taste

Cooking Directions:
1. Set the oven to 400 degrees F to preheat.
2. Cut out 3 sheets of aluminum foil, each large enough to completely cover one cod fillet.
3. Place a cod fillet on each sheet of aluminum foil then add the butter and garlic. Add the bok choy, then season everything with salt and pepper.
4. Fold over the pouches and crimp the edges. Arrange on a baking sheet.
5. Bake for 20 minutes, then transfer to a cooling rack. Let cool slightly, then refrigerate for up to 3 days. Reheat in the oven before serving.

Nutritional Facts per Serving:

Energy (calories)	355	kcal
Protein	37	g

Fat	21	g
Net Carbohydrates	3	g
Fiber	1	g
Sugars, total	1	g

Recipe #8: Creamy Chicken Soup

Number of Servings: 4
Serving Size: 1 cup

Prep Time: 15 minutes
Cook Time: 20 minutes

Ingredients:

- 1 large yellow onion, peeled and diced
- 2 cups organic chicken broth
- 1 cup diced cooked chicken breast
- ½ cup macadamia nuts
- ½ cup water
- ½ cup sliced celery
- ¼ cup diced carrot
- ¼ cup olive oil
- Sea salt, to taste
- Dried herbs de Provence, to taste

Cooking Directions:

1. Place a saucepan over medium flame and heat through. Once hot, add the olive oil and swirl to coat.

2. Sauté the onion, carrot, and celery until the onion is translucent. Then, stir in the macadamia nuts and chicken broth.

3. Bring to a simmer, then reduce to low flame and simmer until the carrot is tender.

4. Turn off the heat and allow the mixture to cool slightly. Then, blend with an immersion blender or high power blender until smooth and the macadamia nuts are pureed. Pour the mixture back into the saucepan.

5. Add ½ cup of water into the soup and stir well to combine. Reheat over medium flame and reheat. Stir in the chicken and stir until reheated.

6. Ladle the soup into individual bowls and allow to cool slightly. Cover and refrigerate for up to 3 days. Reheat before serving.

Nutritional Facts per Serving:

Energy (calories)	325	kcal
Protein	14	g
Fat	28	g
Net Carbohydrates	7	g
Fiber	3	g
Sugars, total	3	g

Recipe #9: Ginger Sesame Halibut

Number of Servings: 3
Serving Size: 1 halibut fillet

Prep Time: 20 minutes
Cook Time: 20 minutes

Ingredients:
- 3 Alaskan halibut fillets, 8 oz. each
- 1 ½ Tbsp. minced fresh ginger
- 1 ½ tsp. soy sauce
- 1 ½ tsp. olive oil
- ¾ tsp. sesame oil
- ¾ tsp. rice wine vinegar

Cooking Directions:
1. Set the oven to 400 degrees F to preheat. Line a baking sheet with aluminum foil and set aside.
2. Combine the sesame and olive oils in a bowl, then stir in the rice vinegar, soy sauce, and ginger.
3. Add the fish fillets and turn several times to coat.
4. Arrange the fish fillets on the prepared baking sheet. Bake for 17 minutes, or until done.
5. Cover each fish fillet with aluminum foil and refrigerate for up to 3 days, or freeze for up to 2 weeks. Reheat before serving.

Nutritional Facts per Serving:
Energy (calories)   237   kcal

Protein	33	g
Fat	35	g
Net Carbohydrates	1	g
Fiber	0.1	g
Sugars, total	0.6	g

Recipe #10: Hearty Beef and Mushroom Stew

Number of Servings: 3
Serving Size: ½ of the recipe

Prep Time: 15 minutes
Cook Time: 50 minutes

Ingredients:

- ½ lb. stew meat, chopped into 1 inch cubes
- ½ lb. sliced baby Portobello mushrooms
- 1 oz. butter
- 2 cups organic beef broth
- ¼ cup extra virgin olive oil
- ¼ cup diced onion
- 2 Tbsp. chopped fresh parsley
- ½ Tbsp. flaxseed meal
- ½ tsp. minced garlic
- ½ tsp. dried thyme
- 1 bay leaf
- Sea salt, to taste
- Freshly ground black pepper, to taste

Cooking Directions:

1. Place a heavy duty pot over medium high flame and heat through. Once hot, add the butter and olive oil and swirl to coat.

2. Add the beef and sauté until all the sides are browned. Then, stir in the mushroom and onion. Sauté until the mushroom is tender and the onion is translucent.

3. Pour in the broth, garlic, bay leaf, thyme, and flaxseed meal then stir to combine. Mix well and bring to a boil.

4. Once boiling, reduce to low flame, cover, and simmer for 45 minutes, or until the beef is extra tender.

5. After 1 hour, discard the bay leaf. Shred the beef using two forks then stir in the parsley. Divide between two airtight containers and refrigerate for up to 3 days. Reheat before serving.

Nutritional Facts per Serving:

Energy (calories)	430	kcal
Protein	25	g
Fat	28	g
Net Carbohydrates	19	g
Fiber	3	g
Sugars, total	2	g

Recipe #11: Goat Cheese and Smoked Onion Pizza

Number of Servings: 4
Serving Size: 1/8 per serving

Prep Time: 20 minutes
Cook Time: 12 minutes

Ingredients:

- 8 large egg whites
- 2 garlic cloves, minced
- 1 ½ cups crumbled goat cheese
- 1 cup chopped yellow onion
- ½ cup coconut milk
- ¼ cup coconut flour
- 4 Tbsp. organic barbecue sauce, no sugar added
- ¼ tsp. baking powder
- ½ tsp. onion powder
- ½ tsp. garlic powder'
- Freshly ground black pepper, to taste

Cooking Directions:

1. Set the oven to 425 degrees F to preheat.
2. Combine the coconut flour, baking powder, and garlic and onion powders in a large bowl.
3. Add the egg whites and coconut milk then stir until smooth.
4. Place a skillet over medium high flame and heat through. Once hot, add ¼ of the mixture and tilt until a flat "pizza crust" is formed.
5. Cook for 2 minutes per side, or until browned. Transfer to a baking sheet and repeat with the remaining batter.

6. Divide the barbecue sauce among the pizza crusts and top with onion, garlic, goat cheese, and a dash of black pepper.

7. Bake the pizzas for 5 minutes, or until the cheese is melted.

8. Transfer to a cooling rack and let cool. Then, wrap in aluminum foil and refrigerate for up to 3 days or freeze for up to 2 weeks. Reheat in the oven or microwave before serving.

Nutritional Facts per Serving:

Energy (calories)	565	kcal
Protein	36	g
Fat	38	g
Net Carbohydrates	13	g
Fiber	4	g
Sugars, total	8	g

Recipe #12: Savory Butternut Squash Soup

Number of Servings: 4
Serving Size: ¾ cup

Prep Time: 15 minutes
Cook Time: 30 minutes

Ingredients:

- ½ lb. butternut squash, peeled, seeded, and cubed
- 1 bay leaf
- 2 garlic cloves, peeled and minced
- 2 cups organic chicken broth
- ¼ cup 36 percent heavy cream
- 2 ½ Tbsp. olive oil
- ½ tsp. fine sea salt

Cooking Directions:

1. Place a saucepan over medium flame and heat through. Once hot, add ½ tablespoon of olive oil and swirl to coat.
2. Stir the butternut squash and garlic into the saucepan and sauté for about 5 minutes or until the garlic is lightly toasted.
3. Pour the chicken broth into the saucepan along with the remaining olive oil. Add the bay leaf, then bring to a boil. Once boiling, reduce to a simmer.
4. Simmer the mixture for about 20 minutes or until the butternut squash is completely tender.
5. Take out and discard the bay leaf, then turn off the heat and allow to cool slightly. Once cooled, blend using an immersion blender or high power blender until smooth.

6. Pour in the cream and blend again until smooth. Then, return to the saucepan and reheat over medium low flame.

7. Season the soup to taste with salt then divide into individual servings. Allow to cool slightly then seal tightly. Refrigerate for up to 3 days. Reheat before serving.

Nutritional Facts per Serving:

Energy (calories)	136	kcal
Protein	2	g
Fat	12	g
Net Carbohydrates	8	g
Fiber	1	g
Sugars, total	2	g

Chapter 6 – Keto Meal Prep Snack Recipes

Recipe #1: Avocado, Cream Cheese and Cucumber Bites

Number of Servings: 5

Serving Size: 2 pieces

Prep Time: 15 minutes

Ingredients:

- 1 large cucumber, sliced into 10 1/3 inch rounds
- 1 large avocado
- 8 oz. cream cheese
- 4 oz. red salmon, flaked
- 1 Tbsp. freshly squeezed lemon juice
- ½ Tbsp. chopped green onion
- Tabasco sauce, to taste

Cooking Directions:

1. Halve the avocado then discard the stone. Scoop out the flesh then place in a large bowl.
2. Mash the avocado and cream cheese together until everything is smooth. Add the lemon juice and mix well, then season to taste with tabasco sauce.
3. Arrange the cucumber slices on a platter then divide the avocado cream cheese mixture among them.

4. Divide the flaked red salmon among the pieces then garnish with green onion. Serve right away, or store in an airtight container and refrigerate for up to 3 days.

Nutritional Facts per Serving:

Energy (calories)	277	kcal
Protein	19	g
Fat	22	g
Net Carbohydrates	5	g
Fiber	3	g
Sugars, total	2	g

Recipe #2: Ham 'n' Cheese Puffs

Number of Servings: 9
Serving Size: 2 puffs

Prep Time: 15 minutes
Cook Time: 30 minutes

Ingredients:
- 6 large eggs
- 10 oz. sliced deli ham, diced
- 1 ½ cups shredded cheddar cheese
- ¾ cup mayonnaise
- 1/3 cup coconut flour
- 1/3 cup coconut oil
- 1/3 tsp. baking powder
- 1/3 tsp. baking soda
- Nonstick cooking spray, as needed

Cooking Directions:
1. Set the oven to 350 degrees F to preheat. Lightly coat rimmed baking sheet with nonstick cooking spray and set aside.
2. In a bowl, mix together the eggs, coconut oil, and mayonnaise. Set aside.
3. In a separate bowl, combine the baking soda, baking powder, and coconut flour. Add the dry ingredients to the wet ingredients and mix well until smooth.
4. Fold the ham and cheddar cheese into the mixture and set aside.
5. Divide the dough into 18 small pieces and arrange on the prepared baking sheet.
6. Bake for 30 minutes, or until the puffs are golden brown and set.
7. Arrange the puffs on a cooling rack and allow to cool slightly.

8. Store into an airtight container for up to 5 days. If desired, reheat in the microwave before serving.

Nutritional Facts per Serving:

Energy (calories)	249	kcal
Protein	15	g
Fat	20	g
Net Carbohydrates	3	g
Fiber	0.3	g
Sugars, total	0.5	g

Recipe #3: Walnut Parmesan Bites

Number of Servings: 10
Serving Size: 4 crackers

Prep Time: 10 minutes
Cook Time: 8 minutes

Ingredients:

- 6 oz. freshly grated Parmesan cheese
- 2 Tbsp. chopped walnuts
- 1 Tbsp. unsalted butter
- ½ Tbsp. chopped fresh thyme

Cooking Directions:

1. Set the oven to 350 degrees F to preheat. Line two large rimmed baking sheets with baking paper and set aside.
2. In a food processor, combine the Parmesan cheese and butter. Blend until combined.
3. Pour in the walnuts and pulse until crushed and combined with the mixture.
4. Using a tablespoon, scoop the mixture onto the prepared baking sheets, then top with chopped thyme.
5. Bake for about 8 minutes, or until golden brown.
6. Transfer to a cooling rack and let set for about 30 minutes. Then, transfer to an airtight container and store for up to 5 days.

Nutritional Facts per Serving:

Energy (calories)	80	kcal
Protein	7	g

Fat	3	g
Net Carbohydrates	7	g
Fiber	0.1	g
Sugars, total	0.2	g

Recipe #4: Cream Cheese Bacon Stuffed Jalapenos

Number of Servings: 4
Serving Size: 2

Prep Time: 15 minutes
Cook Time: 10 minutes

Ingredients:
- 12 large jalapeno peppers
- 16 bacon strips
- 6 oz. full fat cream cheese
- 2 tsp. garlic powder
- 1 tsp. chili powder

Cooking Directions:

1. Set the oven to 350 degrees F to preheat. Place a wire rack over a roasting pan and set aside.
2. Put on a pair of plastic gloves.
3. Make a slit lengthways across the jalapeno peppers, taking care not to cut through. Scrape out and discard the seeds. Set aside.
4. Place a nonstick or cast iron skillet over high flame and heat through. Once hot, add half the bacon strips and cook until crispy. Transfer to a plate lined with paper towels and let drain.
5. Chop the cooked bacon strips and place in a large bowl. Add the cream cheese and mix well to combine.
6. Season the cream cheese and bacon mixture with garlic and chili powder, then mix well.
7. Stuff the jalapeno peppers with the cream cheese mixture, then wrap a raw bacon strip around each pepper.

8. Arrange the stuffed jalapeno peppers on the prepared wire rack, then roast for up to 10 minutes, or until tender.

9. Transfer the stuffed jalapeno peppers on a cooling rack and allow to cool slightly. Transfer to an airtight container and refrigerate for up to 5 days.

Nutritional Facts per Serving:

Energy (calories)	209	kcal
Protein	9	g
Fat	13	g
Net Carbohydrates	19	g
Fiber	3	g
Sugars, total	10	g

Recipe #5: Low Carb Guacamole

Number of Servings: 6
Serving Size: 1/6 of the recipe

Prep Time: 15 minutes

Ingredients:
- 3 large ripe avocados
- 1 large red onion, peeled and diced
- 4 Tbsp. freshly squeezed lime juice
- Sea salt, to taste
- Freshly ground black pepper, to taste
- Cayenne pepper, to taste

Cooking Directions:
1. Halve the avocados then discard the stone.
2. Scoop out the avocado flesh from 3 avocado halves and place in a large glass bowl. Mash well with a fork or potato masher.
3. Add 2 tablespoons of lime juice into the mashed avocado and mix well.
4. Dice the remaining avocado then place in a separate bowl. Add the remaining lime juice and toss gently to coat.
5. Combine the diced avocado with the mashed avocado, then add the chopped onion. Toss again to combine.
6. Season the guacamole with salt, pepper, and cayenne pepper then mix gently to combine.
7. Store in an airtight container for up to 3 days. Serve with carrot, celery, and cucumber sticks.

Nutritional Facts per Serving:

Energy (calories)	172	kcal
Protein	2	g
Fat	15	g
Net Carbohydrates	11	g
Fiber	7	g
Sugars, total	2	g

Recipe #6: Smoked Salmon and Dill Spread

Number of Servings: 8

Serving Size: 2 tablespoons

Prep Time: 20 minutes

Ingredients:

- 4 oz. smoked salmon
- 4 oz. full fat cream cheese, at room temperature
- 2 ½ Tbsp. mayonnaise
- 2 Tbsp. chopped fresh dill
- Sea salt, to taste
- Freshly ground black pepper, to taste

Cooking Directions:

1. Pour the smoked salmon, mayonnaise, and cream cheese into a food processor. Pulse until combined.

2. Pour the mixture into an airtight container and mix in the fresh dill. Season to taste with salt and pepper.

3. Cover and refrigerate for up to 3 days. Best served with carrot, celery, and cucumber sticks.

Nutritional Facts per Serving:

Energy (calories)	70	kcal
Protein	5	g
Fat	5	g
Net Carbohydrates	2	g

Fiber   0.4 g

Sugars, total   0.8 g

Recipe #7: Coco Lime Fat Bombs

Number of Servings: 8
Serving Size: 1 fat bomb

Prep Time: 1 hour 15 minutes

Ingredients:

- 1 oz. cream cheese
- 2 Tbsp. butter
- 2 Tbsp. coconut oil
- 2 Tbsp. heavy cream
- 1 Tbsp. freshly squeezed lime juice
- ½ tsp. lime extract
- ½ tsp. liquid stevia

Cooking Directions:

1. Combine the cream cheese, coconut oil, and butter in a microwaveable bowl. Microwave for 10 seconds three times until melted.
2. Stir the mixture then add the heavy cream. Mix well, then add the lime juice, lime extract, and liquid stevia. Stir well.
3. Pour the mixture into an ice cube tray with 8 compartments. Freeze for at least 1 hour. Store in the freezer for up to 2 weeks. Serve chilled.

Nutritional Facts per Serving:

Energy (calories)	81	kcal
Protein	0.4	g
Fat	9	g

Net Carbohydrates	0.4	g
Fiber	0.4	g
Sugars, total	0.4	g

Recipe #8: Coco Lemon Fat Bombs

Number of Servings: 8

Serving Size: 1 fat bomb

Prep Time: 1 hour 15 minutes

Ingredients:

- 1 oz. cream cheese
- 2 Tbsp. butter
- 2 Tbsp. coconut oil
- 2 Tbsp. heavy cream
- 1 Tbsp. freshly squeezed lemon juice
- ½ tsp. lemon extract
- ½ tsp. liquid stevia

Cooking Directions:

4. Combine the cream cheese, coconut oil, and butter in a microwaveable bowl. Microwave for 10 seconds three times until melted.

5. Stir the mixture then add the heavy cream. Mix well, then add the lemon juice, lemon extract, and liquid stevia. Stir well.

6. Pour the mixture into an ice cube tray with 8 compartments. Freeze for at least 1 hour. Store in the freezer for up to 2 weeks. Serve chilled.

Nutritional Facts per Serving:

Energy (calories)	81	kcal
Protein	0.4	g
Fat	9	g

Net Carbohydrates	0.4	g
Fiber	0.4	g
Sugars, total	0.4	g

Recipe #9: Choco Peanut Fat Bombs

Number of Servings: 8

Serving Size: 1 fat bomb

Prep Time: 1 hour 15 minutes

Ingredients:

- 2 Tbsp. butter
- 2 Tbsp. coconut oil
- 2 Tbsp. heavy cream
- 1 Tbsp. smooth peanut butter
- 1 Tbsp. unsweetened cocoa powder
- ½ tsp. pure vanilla extract
- ½ tsp. liquid stevia

Cooking Directions:

1. Combine the peanut butter, coconut oil, and butter in a microwaveable bowl. Microwave for 10 seconds three times until melted.

2. Stir the mixture then add the heavy cream. Mix well, then add the cocoa powder, vanilla extract, and liquid stevia. Stir well.

3. Pour the mixture into an ice cube tray with 8 compartments. Freeze for at least 1 hour. Store in the freezer for up to 2 weeks. Serve chilled.

Nutritional Facts per Serving:

Energy (calories)	73	kcal
Protein	0.6	g
Fat	8	g

Net Carbohydrates	1	g
Fiber	0.5	g
Sugars, total	0.5	g

Recipe #10: Almond Olive and Herb Tapenade

Number of Servings: 8

Serving Size: 2 tablespoons

Prep Time: 15 minutes

Ingredients:

- 2 garlic cloves, peeled and minced
- 1 cup pitted green olives
- ¼ cup slivered almonds
- ¼ cup packed fresh basil leaves
- ¼ cup extra virgin olive oil
- ½ Tbsp. freshly squeezed lemon juice
- ½ tsp. drained capers
- Sea salt, to taste

Cooking Directions:

1. Combine the almonds, garlic, olives, capers, and lemon juice in a food processor. Pulse until shredded.
2. Add the basil leaves into the food processor and pulse again until combined.
3. Pour in the olive oil and add a dash of salt. Pulse again until the mixture turns into a chunky paste.
4. Pour the mixture into an airtight container and refrigerate for up to 5 days. Best served with grilled chicken tenders or pan-seared white fish strips.

Nutritional Facts per Serving:

Energy (calories)	28	kcal
Protein	0.1	g

Fat	3	g
Net Carbohydrates	0.36	g
Fiber	0.1	g
Sugars, total	0.04	g

Recipe #11: Chocolate Coated Bacon

Number of Servings: 6
Serving Size: 2 pieces

Prep Time: 15 minutes
Cook Time: 20 minutes

Ingredients:
- 12 bacon slices
- 4 ½ Tbsp. unsweetened dark chocolate
- 2 ¼ Tbsp. coconut oil
- 1 ½ tsp. liquid stevia

Cooking Directions:
1. Set the oven to 425 degrees F to preheat.
2. Skewer the bacon in iron skewers, spreading the bacon out.
3. Arrange on a baking sheet. Bake for 15 minutes, or until crisp.
4. Transfer the bacon to a cooling rack and allow to cool completely.
5. Melt the coconut oil in a saucepan over low flame, then stir in the chocolate until melted. Add the stevia and stir well to combine.
6. Place the bacon on a sheet of parchment paper and coat in the chocolate mixture on both sides.
7. Allow the chocolate to dry on the bacon, then transfer the bacon to an airtight container and refrigerate for up to 5 days.

Nutritional Facts per Serving:

Energy (calories)	258	kcal
Protein	7	g

Fat	26	g
Net Carbohydrates	0.5	g
Fiber	0	g
Sugars, total	0.4	g

Recipe #12: Portobello Mushrooms Stuffed with Ricotta Cheese and Spinach

Number of Servings: 6
Serving Size: 1 stuffed mushroom

Prep Time: 15 minutes
Cook Time: 45 minutes

Ingredients:

- 6 large Portobello mushroom caps
- 3 garlic cloves, peeled and minced
- 2 small eggs
- 1 ¼ cups full fat ricotta cheese
- ¾ cup steamed spinach, drained
- ¾ cup freshly grated Parmesan cheese
- ½ cup extra virgin olive oil
- Sea salt, to taste
- Freshly ground black pepper, to taste

Cooking Directions:

1. Set the oven to 425 degrees F to preheat. Line a baking sheet with aluminum foil and set aside.

2. Rinse and clean the Portobello mushroom caps thoroughly until all the dirt is washed off. discard the gills and stems, then blot the mushroom caps with paper towels.

3. Season the inside of the mushroom caps with salt and pepper, then arrange on the prepared baking sheet.

4. Bake the mushroom caps for 15 minutes.

5. Meanwhile, combine the rest of the ingredients in a large bowl until completely combined. Set aside.

6. Remove the mushroom caps out of the oven and then divide the filling among them. Return to the oven and bake for an additional 25 minutes, or until the mushrooms are browned and tender.

7. Place the stuffed mushroom caps on a cooling rack and allow to cool slightly. Serve warm.

8. Store in an airtight container and refrigerate for up to 3 days. Reheat in the microwave oven before serving.

Nutritional Facts per Serving:

Energy (calories)	239	kcal
Protein	16	g
Fat	17	g
Net Carbohydrates	12	g
Fiber	3	g
Sugars, total	3	g

Recipe #13: Cinnamon Butter

Number of Servings: 8
Serving Size: 1 tablespoon

Prep Time:
Cook Time:

Ingredients:

- ½ cup butter, at room temperature
- 5 drops liquid stevia
- ½ tsp. pure vanilla extract
- ½ tsp. ground cinnamon
- 1/8 tsp fine sea salt

Cooking Directions:

1. Combine the butter, vanilla, cinnamon, salt, and stevia in a large bowl. Mix well until smooth.
2. Line a baking sheet with wax paper then spread the cinnamon butter mixture on top. Roll the paper to seal the butter mixture, then seal the ends.
3. Refrigerate the butter for 1 hour before using. Store in the refrigerator for up to 2 weeks. Best served on the Keto Bread or with celery sticks.

Nutritional Facts per Serving:

Energy (calories)	103	kcal
Protein	0.1	g
Fat	12	g
Net Carbohydrates	0.1	g

Fiber	0	g
Sugars, total	0.1	g

Recipe #14: Roasted Eggplant Spread

Number of Servings: 8
Serving Size: 2 tablespoons

Prep Time: 15 minutes
Cook Time: 1 hour

Ingredients:
- 1 lb. eggplant
- 2 ½ Tbsp. chopped roasted red peppers
- 2 Tbsp. extra virgin olive oil
- 2 Tbsp. pine nuts
- 1 Tbsp. freshly squeezed lemon juice
- ½ Tbsp. crumbled feta cheese
- Sea salt, to taste
- Freshly ground black pepper, to taste
- Garlic powder, to taste

Cooking Directions:

1. Set the oven to 400 degrees F to preheat. Slice the eggplant lengthwise in half, then arrange on a baking sheet lined with baking powder.

2. Roast the eggplant for 1 hour, or until extra tender. Then, transfer to a cooling rack and allow to cool slightly.

3. Once cooled, scrape the eggplant flesh out of the skin and place in a food processor. Add the olive oil, red peppers, lemon juice, and pine nuts. Then, blend until smooth.

4. Transfer the eggplant mixture into a bowl and season to taste with salt, pepper, and garlic powder.

5. Sprinkle the crumbled feta cheese over the eggplant mixture and fold in well. Transfer to an airtight container and refrigerate for up to 5 days. Serve with carrot, celery, and cucumber sticks.

Nutritional Facts per Serving:

Energy (calories)	54	kcal
Protein	2	g
Fat	4	g
Net Carbohydrates	4	g
Fiber	2	g
Sugars, total	2.5	g

Recipe #15: Cauli Cheddar Bites

Number of Servings: 6
Serving Size: 6 pieces

Prep Time: 15 minutes
Cook Time: 1 hour and 30 minutes

Ingredients:
- 1 large cauliflower, broken into small florets
- 4 large egg whites
- ½ cup freshly grated strong cheddar cheese
- 2 Tbsp. heavy cream
- 2 Tbsp. butter
- Sea salt, to taste
- Freshly ground black pepper, to taste
- Paprika, to taste
- Nonstick cooking spray

Cooking Directions:

1. Place the cauliflower florets into a pot and add just enough water to cover the base of the pot. Season with salt to taste.

2. Place the pot of cauliflower over high flame and bring to a high simmer. Cook until the cauliflower is tender.

3. Drain the cauliflower florets then transfer to a food processor. Add the heavy cream and butter then blend until the mixture becomes a thick mixture.

4. Season the mixture with salt and pepper, then set aside to cool.

5. Meanwhile, beat the egg whites until soft peaks form. Then, fold in the cauliflower mixture and mix until evenly combined.

6. Add the cheddar cheese to the mixture and fold well until combined.

7. Cover the bowl and refrigerate the mixture for 30 minutes, or until chilled.

8. Set the oven to 375 degrees F to preheat. Lightly coat two rimmed baking sheets with nonstick cooking spray and set aside.

9. Take the cauliflower mixture out of the refrigerator. Using a tablespoon, scoop the mixture onto the prepared baking sheets into bite-sized balls. Ensure there is about 1 ½ inches of space between them.

10. Bake for 30 minutes, or until the bites are golden brown and crisp. Then, transfer to a cooling rack and sprinkle with paprika.

11. Store in an airtight container and refrigerate for up to 5 days. If desired, reheat in a toaster oven before serving.

Nutritional Facts per Serving:

Energy (calories)	142	kcal
Protein	8	g
Fat	10	g
Net Carbohydrates	7	g
Fiber	3	g
Sugars, total	3	g

Recipe #16: Bacon Mozzarella Sticks

Number of Servings: 4
Serving Size: 2 mozzarella sticks

Prep Time: 10 minutes
Cook Time: 5 minutes

Ingredients:

- 8 bacon strips
- 4 mozzarella string cheese pieces
- Sunflower oil, as needed

Cooking Directions:

1. Place a heavy duty skillet over medium flame and add about 2 inches of oil. Heat to 350 degrees F.
2. Meanwhile, halve each string cheese to make 8 pieces.
3. Wrap each piece of string cheese with a strip of bacon and secure with a wooden toothpick.
4. Cook the mozzarella sticks in the preheated oil for 2 minutes, or until the bacon is browned and cooked through.
5. Place the sticks on a plate lined with paper towels and let drain. Transfer to an airtight container and store in the refrigerator for up to 3 days. Reheat before serving.

Nutritional Facts per Serving:

Energy (calories)	278	kcal
Protein	32	g
Fat	15	g

Net Carbohydrates	3	g
Fiber	2	g
Sugars, total	2	g

Chapter 7 – Keto Meal Prep Smoothie Recipes

Recipe #1: Creamy Matcha Green Tea Smoothie

Number of Servings: 2
Serving Size: ½ of the recipe

Prep Time: 10 minutes

Ingredients:

- 1 cup crushed ice
- 1 cup unsweetened almond milk
- ¼ cup heavy cream
- 3 Tbsp. unsweetened vanilla protein powder
- 1 Tbsp. coconut oil
- 1 ½ tsp. green tea powder

Cooking Directions:

1. Combine all the ingredients inside a high powder blender.
2. Blend on low until all ingredients are combined. Then, increase to high speed and blend until smooth.
3. Add a few drops of liquid stevia to taste, then divide into three equal servings. Best served right away.
4. Store extra servings in airtight mason jars and refrigerate for up to 3 days.

Nutritional Facts per Serving:

Energy (calories)	442	kcal
Protein	17	g
Fat	41	g
Net Carbohydrates	7	g
Fiber	3	g
Sugars, total	4	g

Recipe #2: Peanut Butter Choco Smoothie

Number of Servings: 3
Serving Size: 12 oz.

Prep Time: 5 minutes

Ingredients:

- 84 grams whey protein powder
- 3 cups water
- ¾ cup full fat unsweetened coconut milk
- 3 Tbsp. and ¾ tsp. coconut oil
- 3 Tbsp. unsweetened organic peanut butter
- 3 Tbsp. cacao powder
- Liquid stevia, to taste

Cooking Directions:

5. Combine all the ingredients inside a high powder blender.
6. Blend on low until all ingredients are combined. Then, increase to high speed and blend until smooth.
7. Add a few drops of liquid stevia to taste, then divide into three equal servings. Best served right away.
8. Store extra servings in airtight mason jars and refrigerate for up to 3 days.

Nutritional Facts per Serving:

Energy (calories)	371	kcal
Protein	22	g
Fat	25	g

Net Carbohydrates	18	g
Fiber	2	g
Sugars, total	4	g

Recipe #3: Super Berry Almond Smoothie

Number of Servings: 2
Serving Size: ½ of the recipe

Prep Time: 10 minutes

Ingredients:

- 1 cup crushed ice
- ½ cup unsweetened almond milk
- ½ cup frozen raspberries
- ½ cup frozen blueberries
- ½ cup blackberries or strawberries
- 1 Tbsp. coconut oil
- ½ tsp. pure vanilla extract

Cooking Directions:

1. Combine all the ingredients inside a high powder blender.
2. Blend on low until all ingredients are combined. Then, increase to high speed and blend until smooth.
3. Add a few drops of liquid stevia to taste, then divide into three equal servings. Best served right away.
4. Store extra servings in airtight mason jars and refrigerate for up to 3 days.

Nutritional Facts per Serving:

Energy (calories)	252	kcal
Protein	3	g
Fat	22	g

Net Carbohydrates	16	g
Fiber	6	g
Sugars, total	10	g

Recipe #4: Strawberries and Cream Smoothie

Number of Servings: 2

Serving Size: ½ of the recipe

Prep Time: 10 minutes

Ingredients:
- 1 cup crushed ice
- ½ cup sliced and hulled strawberries
- ½ cup heavy cream
- ¼ cup unsweetened almond milk
- 1 Tbsp. coconut oil
- 1 tsp. pure vanilla extract

Cooking Directions:
1. Combine all the ingredients inside a high powder blender.
2. Blend on low until all ingredients are combined. Then, increase to high speed and blend until smooth.
3. Add a few drops of liquid stevia to taste, then divide into three equal servings. Best served right away.
4. Store extra servings in airtight mason jars and refrigerate for up to 3 days.

Nutritional Facts per Serving:

Energy (calories)	249	kcal
Protein	2	g
Fat	25	g
Net Carbohydrates	6	g

Fiber	1	g
Sugars, total	4	g

Recipe #5: Pumpkin Spice Smoothie

Number of Servings: 2

Serving Size: 6 oz.

Prep Time: 10 minutes

Ingredients:

- 2 scoops vanilla whey protein powder
- 1 cup ice cubes
- 1 cup pureed pumpkin
- 1 cup unsweetened vanilla almond milk
- 1 cup ice water
- 1 tsp. pumpkin pie spice
- ¼ tsp. ground cinnamon
- 2 oz. cream cheese
- Liquid stevia, to taste

Cooking Directions:

1. Combine all the ingredients inside a high powder blender.
2. Blend on low until all ingredients are combined. Then, increase to high speed and blend until smooth.
3. Add a few drops of liquid stevia to taste, then divide into three equal servings. Best served right away.
4. Store extra servings in airtight mason jars and refrigerate for up to 3 days.

Nutritional Facts per Serving:

Energy (calories)	268	kcal
Protein	29	g

Fat	10.5	g
Net Carbohydrates	9.5	g
Fiber	3	g
Sugars, total	6	g

Recipe #6: Zesty Green Smoothie

Number of Servings: 3
Serving Size: 6 oz.

Prep Time: 10 minutes

Ingredients:

- ½ avocado, pitted and peeled
- 7 oz. full fat unsweetened coconut milk
- 1 cup chopped baby kale
- ½ cup diced cucumber
- 2 Tbsp. freshly squeezed lemon juice
- 2 Tbsp. freshly squeezed orange juice
- Water, as needed

Cooking Directions:

1. Combine all the ingredients inside a high powder blender.
2. Blend on low until all ingredients are combined. Then, increase to high speed and blend until smooth.
3. Add a few drops of liquid stevia to taste, then divide into three equal servings. Best served right away.
4. Store extra servings in airtight mason jars and refrigerate for up to 3 days.

Nutritional Facts per Serving:

Energy (calories)	218	kcal
Protein	3	g
Fat	21	g

Net Carbohydrates	9	g
Fiber	4	g
Sugars, total	4	g

Recipe #7: Chia Seeds and Crisp Greens Smoothie

Number of Servings: 2

Serving Size: ½ of the recipe

Prep Time: 10 minutes

Ingredients:

- 1 ½ cups crushed ice
- 1 cup packed kale leaves, rinsed thoroughly
- ½ cup water
- ½ cup packed Swiss chard leaves, rinsed thoroughly
- ½ cup packed spinach leaves, rinsed thoroughly
- 2 Tbsp. chia seeds
- 2 Tbsp. coconut oil

Cooking Directions:

1. Combine all the ingredients inside a high powder blender.
2. Blend on low until all ingredients are combined. Then, increase to high speed and blend until smooth.
3. Add a few drops of liquid stevia to taste, then divide into three equal servings. Best served right away.
4. Store extra servings in airtight mason jars and refrigerate for up to 3 days.

Nutritional Facts per Serving:

Energy (calories)	293	kcal
Protein	8	g
Fat	23	g

Net Carbohydrates	15	g
Fiber	11	g
Sugars, total	3	g

Recipe #8: Buttered Coffee Smoothie

Number of Servings: 2
Serving Size: ½ of the recipe

Prep Time: 10 minutes

Ingredients:
- 2 cups crushed ice
- ½ cup iced coffee
- ½ cup heavy cream
- 3 Tbsp. coconut oil

Cooking Directions:
1. Combine all the ingredients inside a high powder blender.
2. Blend on low until all ingredients are combined. Then, increase to high speed and blend until smooth.
3. Add a few drops of liquid stevia to taste, then divide into three equal servings. Best served right away.
4. Store extra servings in airtight mason jars and refrigerate for up to 3 days.

Nutritional Facts per Serving:

Energy (calories)	486	kcal
Protein	1	g
Fat	55	g
Net Carbohydrates	0.9	g
Fiber	0	g

Sugars, total 0.9 g

Recipe #9: Smooth Vanilla Smoothie

Number of Servings: 2

Serving Size: ½ of the recipe

Prep Time: 10 minutes

Ingredients:

- 1 cup crushed ice
- 1 cup unsweetened almond milk
- ¼ cup heavy cream
- 3 Tbsp. unsweetened vanilla whey protein powder
- 1 Tbsp. coconut oil
- 1 tsp. pure vanilla extract

Cooking Directions:

1. Combine all the ingredients inside a high powder blender.
2. Blend on low until all ingredients are combined. Then, increase to high speed and blend until smooth.
3. Add a few drops of liquid stevia to taste, then divide into three equal servings. Best served right away.
4. Store extra servings in airtight mason jars and refrigerate for up to 3 days.

Nutritional Facts per Serving:

Energy (calories)	448	kcal
Protein	17	g
Fat	41	g
Net Carbohydrates	8	g

| Fiber | 2 | g |
| Sugars, total | 5 | g |

Recipe #10: Avocado Coco Smoothie

Number of Servings: 2

Serving Size: ½ of the recipe

Prep Time: 10 minutes

Ingredients:

- 1 avocado, peeled and pitted
- 1 cup crushed ice
- 1 cup unsweetened full fat coconut milk
- 2 Tbsp. freshly squeezed lime juice
- 1 Tbsp. coconut oil
- 1 Tbsp. unsweetened coconut flakes

Cooking Directions:

1. Combine all the ingredients inside a high powder blender.
2. Blend on low until all ingredients are combined. Then, increase to high speed and blend until smooth.
3. Add a few drops of liquid stevia to taste, then divide into three equal servings. Best served right away.
4. Store extra servings in airtight mason jars and refrigerate for up to 3 days.

Nutritional Facts per Serving:

Energy (calories)	512	kcal
Protein	4	g
Fat	51	g
Net Carbohydrates	13	g

| Fiber | 7 | g |
| Sugars, total | 6 | g |

Chapter 8 – Keto Meal Prep Dessert Recipes

Recipe #1: Keto Choco Brownies

Number of Servings: 12
Serving Size: 1 large or 2 small brownie squares

Prep Time: 15 minutes
Cook Time: 20 minutes

Ingredients:

- 1 scoop chocolate flavored whey protein powder
- 3 medium eggs, beaten
- 6 oz. dark chocolate, 80 percent
- ¾ cup unsweetened cocoa powder
- ¾ cup almond flour
- 1/3 cup coconut flour
- 1/3 cup heavy cream
- 1/3 cup cold water
- 3 Tbsp. unsalted butter
- ¾ Tbsp. baking powder
- 1 ½ tsp. pure vanilla extract

Cooking Directions:

1. Set the oven to 325 degrees F to preheat. Line a 9 x 9 inch square baking pan with baking paper and set aside.

2. In a large bowl, mix together the almond and coconut flours, whey protein powder, and baking powder. Set aside.

3. In a glass bowl, combine the heavy cream, chocolate, water, cocoa powder, and butter. Place over a pot of simmering water and stir until melted and evenly combined.

4. Set the bowl of chocolate aside and allow to cool, then add the pure vanilla extract and mix well. Add the eggs and mix well again to combine.

5. Gradually mix the flour mixture into the chocolate mixture until smooth. Then, transfer to the prepared baking pan.

6. Bake the brownies for 20 minutes, or until the brownies are set, but still gooey and chewy.

7. Transfer the pan to a cooling rack and allow to set for about 15 minutes. Then, slice into 12 large squares or 24 small squares.

8. Store the brownies in an airtight container and refrigerate for up to 5 days. Warm in the oven before serving, if desired.

Nutritional Facts per Serving:

Energy (calories)	156	kcal
Protein	4	g
Fat	12	g
Net Carbohydrates	12	g
Fiber	3	g
Sugars, total	4	g

Recipe #2: No Bake Coconut Macaroons

Number of Servings: 18

Serving Size: 2 maracoons

Prep Time: 2 hours and 20 minutes

Ingredients:

- 1 ½ cups shredded unsweetened coconut
- ¾ cup full fat unsweetened coconut milk
- 2 ¼ tsp. stevia

Cooking Directions:

1. Combine all the ingredients in a bowl until thoroughly mixed.
2. Pack down on the mixture then cover with plastic wrap. Refrigerate for at least 2 hours.
3. Once chilled, scoop the coconut mixture into small balls and arrange in a large airtight container.
4. Cover and keep refrigerated for up to 3 days or freeze for up to 3 weeks. Serve chilled.

Nutritional Facts per Serving:

Energy (calories)	47	kcal
Protein	0.4	g
Fat	5	g
Net Carbohydrates	2	g
Fiber	0.8	g

Sugars, total   0.7   g

Recipe #3: Raspberry Cream Cheese Pops

Number of Servings: 8
Serving Size: 2 pieces

Prep Time: 20 minutes

Ingredients:

- ¼ cup cream cheese
- ¼ cup chopped fresh raspberries
- 4 Tbsp. coconut oil
- 4 Tbsp. heavy cream
- 4 Tbsp. butter
- 1 tsp. pure vanilla extract

Cooking Directions:

1. Mix together the cream cheese, coconut oil, and butter in a bowl. Microwave for three times for 10 seconds per interval, or until the mixture is melted.
2. Carefully remove the bowl from the microwave oven and stir well. Then, stir in the heavy cream and fold in the chopped raspberries.
3. Stir the vanilla extract into the mixture and mix well until evenly combined.
4. Pour the mixture into an ice cube tray with 16 sections. Place in the freezer and freeze for at least 2 hours. Serve chilled. Store in the refrigerator for up to 2 weeks for best flavor.

Nutritional Facts per Serving:

Energy (calories)	166	kcal
Protein	0.8	g
Fat	17	g

Net Carbohydrates	2	g
Fiber	0.3	g
Sugars, total	2	g

Recipe #4: Coco Peanut Butter Bites

Number of Servings: 12
Serving Size: 2 pieces

Prep Time: 15 minutes
Cook Time: 12 minutes

Ingredients:

- 2 medium eggs
- ¾ cup unsweetened peanut butter
- ¾ cup butter, at room temperature
- 4 ½ tsp. stevia
- 3 tsp. coconut flour

Cooking Directions:

1. Set the oven to 350 degrees F to preheat. Line a baking sheet with baking paper and set aside.
2. In a large bowl for an electric mixer, combine the peanut butter, butter, eggs, stevia, and coconut flour. Blend well until smooth with an electric mixer.
3. Using a tablespoon, scoop out 24 pieces of the cookie dough and arrange on the prepared baking sheet.
4. Bake for 12 minutes, or until crisp and golden brown.
5. Place the baking sheet of cookies on a cooling rack and allow to cool completely. Then, transfer to an airtight container and refrigerate for up to 5 days, or store for up to 3 weeks.

Nutritional Facts per Serving:

Energy (calories)　　　159　　kcal

Protein	2	g
Fat	15	g
Net Carbohydrates	4	g
Fiber	0.3	g
Sugars, total	3	g

Recipe #5: Cocoa Nibbles with Cream Cheese

Number of Servings: 6
Serving Size: 4 small pieces

Prep Time: 15 minutes
Cook Time: 10 minutes

Ingredients:

- 2 medium eggs
- 4 oz. melted butter
- 2 oz. full fat cream cheese
- 1 oz. coconut flour
- ½ tsp. baking soda
- ½ tsp. baking powder
- ½ tsp. xanthan gum
- ½ tsp. pure vanilla extract
- ¼ tsp. liquid stevia

Cooking Directions:

1. Set the oven to 350 degrees F to preheat. Line a rimmed baking sheet with baking paper and set aside.

2. In a large bowl, beat the cream cheese and butter until smooth. Set aside.

3. In another bowl, combine the coconut flour, baking soda, baking powder, and xanthan gum. Set aside.

4. In a small bowl, combine the vanilla extract, liquid stevia, and egg, then beat well until smooth.

5. Gradually stir the flour mixture into the cream cheese mixture until well combined. Add the egg mixture and mix well.

6. Using a tablespoon, scoop the mixture onto the prepared baking sheet, making sure there is at least 1 ½ inches between each piece.

7. Bake for 10 minutes, or until the pieces are golden brown around the edges.

8. Transfer to a cooling rack and allow to set for about 10 minutes. Transfer to an airtight container and refrigerate for up to 5 days.

Nutritional Facts per Serving:

Energy (calories)	178	kcal
Protein	3	g
Fat	18	g
Net Carbohydrates	1	g
Fiber	0.1	g
Sugars, total	0.8	g

Recipe #6: Creamy Vanilla Pudding

Number of Servings: 4
Serving Size: ¼ cup

Prep Time: 5 minutes
Cook Time: 12 minutes

Ingredients:

- 2 large egg yolks
- 1 cup 36 percent heavy cream
- 1 ½ tsp. stevia
- 1 tsp. arrowroot flour
- ½ tsp. pure vanilla extract
- Fine sea salt, to taste

Cooking Directions:

1. Combine the egg yolks in a heavy duty saucepan then whisk in the heavy cream, stevia, arrowroot flour, and pure vanilla extract. Mix well.

2. Add a dash of salt and whisk to combine. Then, place over medium flame and stir until the mixture starts to steam.

3. Reduce to low flame and continue to stir for about 10 minutes.

4. After 10 minutes, pour the pudding through a mesh sieve into 4 heatproof containers.

5. Place a sheet of plastic wrap directly on top of the pudding and refrigerate for up to 3 days. Serve chilled.

Nutritional Facts per Serving:

Energy (calories)   135   kcal

Protein	2	g
Fat	13	g
Net Carbohydrates	2	g
Fiber	0	g
Sugars, total	0.9	g

Recipe #7: Lemon Poppy Seed Cupcakes

Number of Servings: 12
Serving Size: 1 cupcake

Prep Time: 15 minutes
Cook Time: 30 minutes

Ingredients:

- 7 large eggs
- 10 oz. full fat plain Greek yogurt
- 4 oz. melted butter
- 3 oz. coconut flour
- 2 ½ Tbsp. freshly squeezed lemon juice
- 2 Tbsp. poppy seeds
- 2 ½ tsp. freshly grated lemon zest
- 2 tsp. baking powder
- 1 tsp. liquid stevia

Cooking Directions:

1. Set the oven to 375 degrees F to preheat. Line 12 cupcake tins with paper liners and set aside.
2. In a large bowl, whisk together the eggs, yogurt, and liquid stevia. Then, add the melted butter and mix well. Set aside.
3. Combine the coconut flour with the baking powder in a separate bowl, then mix into the egg mixture. Stir until smooth.
4. Stir the lemon juice and zest into the batter, followed by the poppy seeds. Stir well until evenly combined.

5. Pour the batter into the prepared cupcake tins, then bake for up to 30 minutes, or until the cupcakes are done. To check for readiness, insert a toothpick into the center of one cupcake; if it comes out done, they are ready.

6. Transfer the cupcakes onto a cooling rack and allow to cool slightly. Transfer to an airtight container and refrigerate for up to 5 days. Reheat in the oven before serving, if desired.

Nutritional Facts per Serving:

Energy (calories)	214	kcal
Protein	10	g
Fat	16	g
Net Carbohydrates	10	g
Fiber	3	g
Sugars, total	2	g

Conclusion

Since you have reached the end of this book, it is safe to assume that you have tried many, if not all, of the recipes in this book and you are probably wondering what to have next. Of course, you can always make modifications to these recipes to give your taste buds variety, and at the same time, make the most out of seasonal ingredients.

You can also continue to add more recipes to this collection so that you would never run out of ideas on what to meal prep in the next 30 days. But with over 70 recipes to choose from, you probably never will!

Thank you!

Before you go, I just wanted to say thank you for purchasing my book.

You could have picked from dozens of other books on the same topic but you took a chance and chose this one.

So, a HUGE thanks to you for getting this book and for reading all the way to the end.

Now I wanted to ask you for a small favor. **Could you please take just a few minutes to leave a review for this book on Amazon?**

This feedback will help me continue to write the type of books that will help you get the results you want. So if you enjoyed it, please let me know! (-:

Book – II
INTERMITTENT FASTING

A Simple, Proven Approach to the Intermittent Fasting Lifestyle - Burn Fat, Build Muscle, Eat What You Want

INTRODUCTION

If you are an avid searcher for methods and techniques that you hopefully think would help you achieve your desired body figure and health, you might have already run into several terms associated with diet and workout like Atkins diet, ketogenic diet, water therapy, and strength training.

There are actually a lot more terms and each of them probably had become a top searched figure at least once. But, there is this one method that is becoming more and more prominent these days, as it continues to prove its effectiveness not only to weight loss but also to the overall health of an individual—the intermittent fasting.

What if I told you that losing weight is not necessarily a matter of "what you eat," but instead a matter of "when you eat?" In this book, you'll find out what intermittent fasting is, and why people who relied on several diet methods before are gradually moving into this method.

This book will guide you throughout your journey; from learning everything about intermittent fasting up to applying the method to your lifestyle. You'll discover the benefits of the method not only as a way to lose fat but also as a means to improve certain functions in your health. There is also a step-by-step, comprehensive guide that will provide all the help you need so you could start on your new weight-loss program.

Get ready for the huge changes in your lifestyle and be prepared for the massive results that await you, as you take your very first step in this life-changing journey to a healthy weight loss!

Part I – Everything You Need to Know About Intermittent Fasting

CHAPTER 1

The Practice of Fasting

Fasting has been one of the most prominent methods of weight loss ever since it was introduced to our history. Up until today, there are a lot of people who prefer using the fasting method to shed some pounds, as they believe it's the best way to lose weight. Some of those who have proven the effectiveness of fasting even call it a "life cheat" or a "life hack" as it provides the result they desire without any cost at all.

There are, however, several claims that discredit the method and prove contrary to what is said to be its effect. Some nutritionists say that fasting is unhealthy and should not be promoted to the public as it can cause nutrition deficiencies and other health-related problems. In spite of this, there are still people who find fasting a great and easy way to lose weight. But, is fasting really just a matter of not eating to reduce body weight?

Fasting, in its purest definition, is the abstinence from consuming foods, drinks, or both for a certain period of time. During the early ages when different religions were still fighting over lands, people, and beliefs, it was not considered a form of diet; but instead, a practice to prove one's faith to the god of whatever religion a man believed. It was more of an obedience rather than a health-related practice.

Nowadays, fasting is still associated with existing religions and is still regarded as a part of religious practices. In Buddhism, monks and nuns strictly abide by the Vinaya rules. They do not eat after the noon meal and they stick to this practice every day. Under Christianity, the practice of fasting is linked to the passages expressly written in the biblical Book of Isaiah. In there, fasting is said to be not only a mere abstinence from food or water but also a decision to fully obey the god's commands. And in Islam, Muslims believe that aside from food abstinence, the practice of "fasting" also entails avoidance of acting and speaking of falsehood.

In the context of physiology and health, fasting refers simply to a person's metabolic status when he has not eaten overnight. It's the metabolic state after a person achieves full digestion and absorption of meal. It usually happens during sleep as this is the phase when the body doesn't receive anything and thus, is focused only on full digestion. From this very description, we can say that fasting is not just one of the thousands of methods of losing weight. It's actually a normal phenomenon that happens to every person, every day.

Just like those of any other practice related to health improvement and diet, the effects of fasting differ from person to person, depending on a variety of factors such as a person's age, current medication he is currently taking, his existing health issues if there are any, and his body's response to hunger. Nonetheless, fasting still has proven its own importance in the field of medicine and medical research.

There are distinguished types into which different ways of fasting are usually categorized namely dry fasting, water fasting, diagnostic fast, and intermittent fasting. All of these types use abstinence from either food or water but vary on their purposes.

Absolute Fast

An absolute fast (also known as dry fasting) is the complete abstinence of food and liquid that lasts commonly for 24 hours. This type of fasting can further be extended up to a couple of days. This is usually a practice done for religious purposes.

Water Fast

This type of fasting is almost like an absolute fasting except that it allows the consumption of drinking water during fasting period; but aside from drinking water, all other liquids are prohibited. This type is believed to be practiced by some people in order to "cleanse" their bodies. The most common diet method associated with this type is the water therapy which has been proven effective in weight-loss procedures.

Diagnostic Fast

Diagnostic fast is a fasting supported by medical practitioners. It is technically a part of medical procedure performed as a pre-observation measure. It is a fasting advised to, and done by people who undergo or will undergo a medical investigation with regard to certain health problems like hypoglycemia. Some procedures also require diagnostic fasting before the actual check-up such as in a colonoscopy.

Intermittent Fast

Intermittent fasting is the type of fasting that is neither absolute nor done for diagnostic purposes. It is seen as an aid in diet and is proven effective for burning fats, building muscle, and controlling nutritional intake. This will be elaborately discussed in the proceeding chapters. There is also a section that will guide you on how to perform intermittent fasting properly and the supplemental things that will help you achieve better results. So, what are you waiting for? Let's proceed to the next chapter!

CHAPTER 2

Intermittent Fasting

They say an apple a day keeps the doctor away, but consuming like seven or more apples each day is not anymore covered by this golden saying.

Eating a lot of healthy foods can surely provide dramatic changes to your overall health. However, "a lot" of these foods could sometimes be "too much" for your body that it wouldn't be able to respond properly anymore; yes, even those foods which are worshipped as the healthiest. This is when intermittent fasting comes in—promoting nutrition regulation and diet control.

But, what exactly is intermittent fasting? Intermittent fasting is an eating or diet schedule which follows a cycle of alternating eating and no-eating periods. A person who practices intermittent fasting basically abides by a schedule that divides the day or the week into fasting and eating periods which are patterned at regular intervals. For example, on a week-based intermittent fasting schedule, a person might assign his Mondays, Wednesdays, and Saturdays as fasting periods, which means he should not eat on those days; and then his Sundays, Tuesdays, Thursdays, and Fridays as his eating periods.

Assigning schedules for intermittent fasting can be as simple as every other day, or as complex as a combination of week-based and day-based fasting—in a day-based fasting, a person splits his daily time frame into eating and fasting periods. In any case, intermittent fasting isn't really that much of a new idea to the body.

As once mentioned in the preceding chapter, the time when a person sleeps can already be considered as fasting time. This is because the body's digestive properties do not have any new substance to digest during sleep; thus, they stop right after fully completing the digestion. The idea of intermittent fasting is simply to extend this portion of time and retain the "empty" state of stomach until the next scheduled eating time. It's almost just like sleeping for a longer period.

How Intermittent Fasting Is Done

Let's say for example, you are planning to start practicing a day-based intermittent fasting. The first thing you want to know is how long your fasting period should be in each day. Ideally, the proper fasting period should be 15 to 16 hours a day; this leaves you nine to eight hours for your eating period. The remaining eight- or nine-hour eating window should strictly be the only time when you are allowed to eat. Majority of those who practice intermittent fasting usually set two meals for this length.

Now that you know both your eating period and fasting period, you need to choose which time should each period start and end. If you are familiar with weight-loss diet plans and protocols, you probably know that the best time at which you can set your dinner is as early as seven or eight in the evening. Let's say that you set your dinner at seven in the evening, counting back eight hours from 7 pm you'll have 11 am. This means that your eating period should start at 11 in the morning and should end at seven in the evening. The rest of the hours that are not covered by your eating window should be a no-eating or -drinking period. If you normally wake up at 8 am then you should skip the breakfast, take your lunch at 11 am, have your dinner at 7 pm and sleep at whatever time you usually go to bed.

Science and Medical Research

Several studies were already done to examine the effectiveness and safety of intermittent fasting. Most of the results of these research studies showed remarks that were close to each other although the proponents and other scientists have not yet come up with a hard and fast conclusion. This is because each result had its own distinct negative impact to the samples; from minor issues to major health problems. Scientists believe that these issues were brought by a lot of factors such as the differences in the health of participants, and the foods, themselves which are offered during eating time. Nevertheless, the positive effects of most of these studies were found to be more dominant than the negative ones. This induces the scientists and researchers to further conduct studies to support this type of fasting.

One of the most prominent and current research done concerning the effects of scheduled or intermittent fasting was a research in endocrinology conducted by proponents from the United States of America. The study called the fasting schedule as intermittent energy restriction or IER. The IER's counterpart was the ad libitum feeding or free feeding. The IER followed the intermittent fasting schedule while the ad libitum feeding simply based the feeding on the sample's own biological hunger phase.

Like in the usual setting of laboratory tests, the first testing was done on rodents. The mice were divided into two groups—the IER group and the free-feeding group. After five months of feeding, both groups were observed and examined. It was found out that among the mice used for testing, those under the IER group showed dramatic reduction from their initial glucose and insulin levels—the examination was a part of a study about type 2 diabetes. Those under the free-feeding group, on the other hand, either retained their original glucose and insulin levels or developed slight changes from their original levels. Either way, it was found out that the glucose and insulin levels of mice in the IER group were significantly lower than those of the mice in the other group.

It was further found out from the same research study that despite having lower glucose and insulin levels, the mice under the IER group were surprisingly not suffering from energy deficiency. The proponents believe that it was because the mice of IER group had already adapted to their new eating setting and they therefore would require only less levels of glucose and insulin intake to suffice their energy needs.

There was also a study that found intermittent fasting as a huge contributory factor when it comes to weight loss. Such study also involved rodents as its subjects. In the first phase of the test, all of the rats had ad libitum access to standard food; they were able to consume meals whenever they felt hungry. The first phase lasted for four weeks. After the fourth week, the rats were then divided into two groups. The first group of rats continued with the ad libitum feeding while the second group underwent strict diet schedule which consisted eating and fasting days, similar to the IER group from the previously mentioned study.

The rats from each group were then further tested for another 10 weeks. After the 10th week, each of the group was examined—it was discovered that there were huge reductions in the body weights of those rats under the second group or the IER group. The differences between the body weights of the rats belonging to the IER group after the first phase of the study and after the second phase, were comparable to those of the rats which belonged to the first group. The results were further examined and brought to an analysis of the IER's efficacy in relation to the development of insulin resistance due to high fat diet.

Intermittent Fasting Effects on Humans

Of course, the previously mentioned pieces of evidence won't be enough to back up even just half of the claimed efficacy of intermittent fasting for these only involved rodents as their subjects. But in the usual research laboratory environment, such tests are relevant and reasonable enough to consider the study as applicable to an upper level form of subject—humans.

One research study featured on an article entitled, Nutrition & Diabetes, suggested that intermittent fasting—coupled with low-energy diet—resulted to improvements on both glucose metabolism and cardiovascular health. The study involved both overweight and obese people. It used IER trial as well and the observation period lasted three months. After the third month of strict diet implementation, the subjects were examined to identify the presence of cardiovascular risk markers and to assess the glucose levels of individuals.

Majority of the subjects showed positive changes on both aspects. There were less risk markers on their cardiovascular health which could lead to serious heart diseases if left maintained at a high level. Plus, their glucose metabolism has improved. The subjects' levels of blood pressure were also examined in the same study although there were minimal inconsistencies when such results are compared to the results of other studies which also focused on the effects of intermittent fasting. Thus, only the IER's effect on cardiovascular health and glucose properties of humans was considered safe to conclude, at least as of the current state.

There was also an intermittent fasting trial performed on non-obese, healthy individuals. In a matter of three weeks, effects became evident on the individuals who took part in the trial. On men participants, triglyceride levels were lowered to a healthier state. Triglyceride is an organic compound which can be found in a human body. The presence of high levels of triglyceride compounds in the body is a sign that an individual is prone to or has diabetes or kidney disease.

With regard to the women participants, the researchers found a post-treatment increase in high-density lipoprotein or HDL cholesterol. HDL cholesterol functions as an important substance in the body as it removes excess cholesterol from the blood, the cells, and the walls of blood vessels; hence, called the good cholesterol. The variation of the effects based on gender is believed to be caused by the level of fasting each gender group naturally possesses; men participants tended to have higher fasting levels than women participants. Though the results of the study were found to be gender-specific, they were considered a helpful tool to demonstrate the positive effects of intermittent fasting.

There are more studies to back up the effects of intermittent fasting but enumerating each would take a lifetime to be thoroughly explained. Besides, the concept of intermittent fasting, being widely accepted as a major topic on health and diet, has just yet begun on getting attention in the field of medical research. That is why the studies related to it are not as numerous and as conclusive as those which have focused on well-known, broader health topics such as diabetes, skin care, or workout trainings.

CHAPTER 3

Benefits of Intermittent Fasting

Even if intermittent fasting sounds like a common practice that has been naturally existing for centuries, the conceptualization of the practice is actually not that old. A number of research studies are still on the line and medical researchers are still either planning or conducting several trials in pursuit of developing a solid conclusion to close the case—which would be more likely to take years or decades to happen.

But as of the studies that are currently on record, intermittent fasting already holds quite a decent impression when it comes to human health. Majority of the past trials ended up with a positive conclusion regarding the beneficial effects of the diet concept to people. These benefits include induced cell repair processes, reduced oxidative stress, lowered insulin resistance, increased brain function and protection, weight loss and muscle growth, as well as increased protection against certain diseases.

Induced Repair Processes on Cells

Fasting prompts the cells in your body to perform autophagy which is the process through which cells undergo self-destruction. Autophagy is a normal physiological phenomenon which is meant to maintain normal cellular functioning. Destroyed cell organelles are turned over for the generation of new cells. This helps the body maintain a healthy set of cells and get rid of unnecessary or damaged organelles which could cause serious diseases such as cancer, when not destroyed.

When an individual does not consume food or water for a prolonged span of time, the stress level in his body increases. A healthily elevated stress level induces autophagy to take place; and this is the exact reason that fasting is considered a biological stressor which brings a healthy amount of positive effects in the body including autophagy.

Reduced Oxidative Stress

Oxidative stress happens when the production of free radicals is not countered by the body's ability to detoxify their negative effects to health. This happens either because there is an abnormally excessive production of free radicals that the body's natural ability, even at a normal state, cannot battle the free radicals' harmful effects; or because the body's antioxidant activity became too weak that it couldn't keep pace even with the normal production of free radicals.

The ability of the body to deter harmful effects of free radicals is called neutralization which is brought by the body's antioxidants. Antioxidants are molecules that safely interact with free radicals, as well as counteract and detoxify their harmful effects, to maintain a healthy set of cells. An imbalance between antioxidant activity and free radical production brings oxidative stress to place; and therefore, damages the components of the cell.

Short-period fasting works by ironically causing a slight increase in free radical production. This triggers the cells in the body to respond on a more secure level by increasing the level of anti-oxidant activity. When this happens, the antioxidants will be able to detoxify all the free radicals and will lessen the oxidative stress.

Lowered Insulin Resistance

Insulin is a hormone produced by the pancreas which extracts glucose from carbohydrates and converts them into energy. It can also store glucose in the body for future use. However, when the body receives too much insulin, it tries to counter this excessive level until it eventually fails to respond properly to the hormone.

Insulin resistance is a serious complication that entails some of the known major health problems. This is because insulin helps keep the body's blood sugar level in regulation. Thus, when the body resists insulin, it also loses its control over blood sugar level; making the body prone to both hyperglycemia or the surge in blood sugar level, or hypoglycemia or the abnormal drop in blood sugar level.

In a certain study involving humans as subjects, intermittent fasting was attributed to a 3-6% decrease in blood sugar and 20-31% drop in insulin level. The figures showed good indications of insulin level improvement. A decrease in insulin level is technically helpful since in the first place, insulin resistance is brought by excessive insulin level. The study also showed that intermittent fasting protected the subjects from kidney damage.

Increased Brain Function and Protection

As of the currently existing studies, though only involving animal samples, intermittent fasting has proven a number of benefits to the brain. One of these studies discovered that the growth of nerve cells on those mice which underwent intermittent fasting, accelerated after the intervention period. Another study showed that intermittent fasting could prevent brain damage that could further lead to stroke.

An increase in brain-derived neurotrophic factor or BDNF was also found evident on the samples involved in a study about dietary restriction and its effects on the brain. Deficiency in BDNF hormones are implicated in various mental health issues including depression.

Weight Loss and Muscle Growth

Among the effects of intermittent fasting, weight loss is what people sought after the most. This type of diet pattern has been used and incorporated in several fitness plans and is becoming more and more trendy among health-conscious people because of its huge impact to the body. Plus, it comes with a bonus—studies show that intermittent fasting helps retain lean mass and promote muscle growth. All of these will be elaborately discussed in the next chapter.

Increased Protection Against Certain Diseases

Due to the previously mentioned benefits, it is apparent that intermittent fasting can safely be attributed to lowered risks of certain types of diseases. The improved cell repair processing can help the body get rid of cancer. The decrease in oxidative stress may battle brain-health issues such as depression and Alzheimer's disease. Improvements in insulin level, on the other hand, are directly connected to insulin resistance and are therefore helpful to combat diabetes as well. Above all, intermittent fasting is an effective tool for a healthier way of losing weight, making it both a preventive and a corrective measure against obesity.

CHAPTER 4

Intermittent Fasting – Key to a Healthy Weight Loss and Muscle Growth

The most probable reason a person follows an intermittent fasting schedule is weight loss. Fortunately, weight loss is among one of the evidence-supported benefits that intermittent fasting promotes. Well, fasting in general promotes weight loss; so, what makes intermittent fasting a different and better option?

When you fast, you basically do not allow your body to receive calories from foods. This means you are not prone to storing excess calories as fats in your body. Therefore, if your body continues to fast, there are only two things that can happen to your body weight—remain as is or decrease. Among the two, it is the latter which is more likely to happen since fats are naturally burned during activities regardless if they are eventually replaced or not.

Although the idea is scientifically true, not all people who tried fasting succeeded in losing weight. As a matter of fact, some of them even ended up gaining more. This is because the general term "fasting" simply means abstaining from foods, drinks, or both. It does not define how much to abstain, for how long one should abstain, nor what happens next after someone starved himself for an unusual length of time—it often ends up being misinterpreted as an unregulated way of skipping at least one full meal.

Most of the people "fast" by skipping breakfast. But when the lunch time comes, they tend to eat more than usual to satisfy the prolonged hunger they endured before the meal. This is the common mistake people do when they fast; they do not pair it with discipline. If you fast for 48 hours, you'll most probably eat a lot on your next meal as your body needs to gain what it didn't during the fasting period; regardless if you try to control it or not. This is why fasting for straight long periods is not recommended by nutritionists and health experts.

Intermittent fasting, on the other hand, follows a uniform cycle of periods; hence, regulated. It gradually lets the body adjust into a new setup until it becomes used to it. It does not abuse hunger too much as it still includes the three main meals of the day, or two at the least. So, there is nothing to worry about not being able to control food intake. The diet concept actually just expands the span of time when your body is not consuming anything and narrows your eating-window. This is considerably a healthy setup if you want to shed some pounds. In here, you are giving your body enough time to fully digest meals so as to absorb the nutrients properly instead of merely storing them as fats.

Accelerated Fat-Burning Process

Moreover, short-period fasting also accelerates your metabolism which means your body can burn more calories when you follow intermittent fasting. In a certain study published by the National Center for Biotechnology Information or NCBI in the US National Library of Medicine, short-term starvation led to an average of 3.6% increase in the metabolic rate of the subjects.

11 healthy young individuals took part in the said study, all of whom are normal-weight. They were not allowed to eat meals for 48 hours. After the intervention period, the metabolic rate of each individual increased in varied rates with a mean of 3.6%. Such number was considered as a large increase in metabolism level and was entirely attributed to the starvation or fasting period.

Intermittent Fasting vs. Daily Calorie Restriction

There exists a traditional diet regimen called daily calorie restriction or CR through which an individual limits his daily calorie intake to a fixed measure. If you adopt this kind of diet technique, you need to be conscious on the quantity of the food you consume and make sure that you do not exceed your calorie limit. So, if let's say, you are only allowed to take 1500 calories per day, your total calorie consumption should not be 1600 or 1700 calories but 1400 calories or below are allowed. This technique has proven favorable results to individuals who practice the CR method but there's one downside to this—it's hard to maintain such kind of diet.

First of all, the meals an individual takes every day usually do not have a readily available calorie measure. And in such case, the individual must rely heavily on estimation which is not a good thing, considering that the very purpose of the CR method is to quantify the exact calorie intake of a person in order to regulate consumption. Unfortunately, approximation is not ideal most especially when you need to implement the diet method in the strictest terms.

Secondly, even if an individual consumes foods and products in boxes or cartons (which most probably have a calorie amount indicator on their nutrition facts sections), it will be hard for an individual to guarantee that what he had just consumed would be equal to the calorie amount that was written on the packaging; say, what if he did not consume all the content? Besides, packed foods are not really the healthiest option for an individual who claims to be "on a diet."

Lastly, it's not always safe to say that a person can control his food intake every day based on a fixed calorie limit. It should not be forgotten that calories are also energy providers and not just "potential" fats. There might come a day which would demand more energy from an individual and choosing to stick with the limited-calorie food intake clearly would not be efficient.

In contrast to the quantified restriction of CR method, intermittent fasting allows free intake of food during eating-windows. This diet schedule is after the lengthening of fasting period and shortening the eating period without necessarily limiting the calorie intake; while the CR method does not restrict consumption based on time but on the size of food, itself. To be honest, both are equally effective in reducing weight but there are recent studies which can back up the claim that intermittent fasting is better than calorie restriction method in some aspects other than mere fat mass reduction.

According to an article published by the Department of Kinesiology and Nutrition of the University of Illinois in Chicago, the intermittent diet schedule may be more effective in retaining the lean mass in the body while reducing weight. The study used obese individuals as subjects. The review focused on examining weight loss as well as the corresponding fat mass loss and lean mass retention. Under the daily CR diet, the average weight loss was 5-8% while the average fat mass loss was 10-20%. On the other hand, the intermittent diet resulted into 4-8% average weight loss and 11-16% fat mass loss.

The figures were evidently near to each type. However, the researchers further identified that although both were effective for weight reduction, the intermittent fasting resulted to a greater retention of lean mass than CR diet. Lean mass, in a nutshell, is the portion in your weight that isn't fat. This portion includes the weight of your bones, your muscles, the water in your body, and technically, all of your organs. This is the reason that a lot of nutritionists advise body builders to go after either retaining or gaining lean mass while reducing fat mass.

Muscle Mass Retention and Growth

An unregulated fasting might be helpful in losing weight but the problem with it is that along the process of shedding fat mass, you might also lose some of your lean mass. This is a crucial matter as a lot of people mistake losing weight as synonymous to being healthy. Unless all the weight you lost is composed of fat mass, it is not safe to say that your body did get healthier.

It is only important to understand that fat loss is different from muscle loss although the tricky part is that, both can happen in a single weight loss activity. If you focus too much on losing weight without keeping track of your muscle health, chances are you'll end up degrading your muscle strength. Since intermittent fasting helps retain lean mass amid weight reduction, it can therefore also help retain muscle mass for body builders.

Retaining muscle mass is just as hard as gaining it. Even if you gained much, it won't make any noticeable change if you also lost much of it at the same time. Let's say for example, you weigh 170 pounds and that you constantly gain two pounds of muscle mass per month because of consistent training. In a span of one year, we can say that you'll gain 24 pounds of lean muscle mass turning your initial 170-pound weight into 194 pounds. That is a huge muscle improvement considering you didn't gain any significant fat mass the whole year. But what if during the year, due to unregulated fasting, you also lost a total of 23 pounds of lean mass? Your weight at the end of the year will then only be 171 pounds—a frustratingly one-pound gain for a whole year of training.

Consistency in growth is the key to build stronger muscles—and to look more ripped in case appearance is a factor. This is why muscle gainers must follow diet patterns which support retention of lean muscle mass. And such rule shall also apply to those who want to lose weight and gain muscle at the same time.

Getting Rid of Belly Fat

If you are one of those people who are overly conscious with their fat tummies and how they keep on showing a bump under your otherwise gorgeous clothes, then there's a good news for you—intermittent fasting is also associated with belly fat reduction.

There was a study regarding the effect of intermittent fasting on type 2 diabetes, which tested individuals with "fat tummies." These individuals underwent intermittent fasting and after 24 weeks, the fasting alone provided the individuals 4-7% waist circumference reduction. This is largely connected to the previously tested efficacy of intermittent fasting when it comes to overall weight loss.

CHAPTER 5

Types of Intermittent Fasting

Several variations of intermittent fasting have already been made even before the diet pattern became popular to the world. And as it gets more and more attention from health enthusiasts and nutritional experts, the list becomes longer. All of the types that exist to date are created out of varying needs so it cannot really be identified which among these "best" fits all. In fact, majority of those who largely benefited from intermittent fasting are using a mixture of two or more of these types.

There are, however, a few types of intermittent fasting that have established a decent impression to both nutritionists and diet experts. These intermittent fasting variants have made it to the list mainly because a number of people found these diet patterns appropriate for them and for their needs.

5:2 Diet

Popularized by British journalist and producer Michael Mosley, this is by far the most prominent kind of intermittent fasting. 5:2 diet is a week-based fasting schedule meaning; a cycle lasts for a week and every cycle or week is split into fasting and eating days. This is a simple schedule that can be followed by anyone and is also among one of the most flexible diet patterns.

5:2 basically means five whole days of free-eating for two full days of fasting. Since a week is composed of seven days, you can just set two of these days as your fasting days and freely consume foods for the rest of the week. On every fasting day, you can only consume a total of not more than 25% of your average daily calorie consumption. Yes, "fasting" here refers to a period of limited intake and not an absolutely no-food nor -drink period; thus, you can still eat but with limitation.

To provide a clearer picture of how 5:2 diet is followed, let's say you designated your Wednesdays and Thursdays as your fasting days. On your Fridays up to your Tuesdays, you can eat your meals the way you normally do; you can eat breakfast, lunch, dinner and even snacks. There are no limits on eating days. On the other hand, your Wednesdays and Thursdays are a little stricter when it comes to your consumption. If your average calorie consumption per day is let's say 2000, your calorie limit would be 500 (2000 multiplied by

25%). This means you should not eat more than 500 calories on your Wednesdays and neither on your Thursdays. Fasting days in 5:2 diet aren't that strict though. You can still have three meals during these days except that the meals would be relatively smaller.

Do your fasting days have to be consecutive days? Well, as stated earlier, 5:2 diet is known for being one of the most flexible diet patterns; so nope, those days do not necessarily have to be consecutive. Majority of the 5:2 diet users find hunger easier to sustain when the two fasting days are apart from each other like Mondays and Wednesdays or Tuesdays and Fridays. It is even highly recommended for beginners to set these periods on non-consecutive days, considering a 75% decrease in one's normal calorie intake is a huge, sudden drop. So, if you want to overcome your first few weeks under 5:2 diet, better refrain from picking two consecutive days. Consecutive days are more convenient though and as long as the fasting won't exceed 48 hours, they are believed to provide equally healthy but slightly faster results.

Another thing that makes it a flexible diet pattern is that each cycle does not have to follow a uniform pattern. This means you can fast on the Thursday and Friday of the current week and switch these fasting days into the Tuesday and Wednesday of the following week. Of course, uniform cycles are better so your body could adapt to consistency but it's much better to stick to reality and consider the possibilities that you can't always be free to fast on the same days of every week. Nonetheless, it is still up to you how you would like to apply this type of intermittent fasting to each of your weeks.

Further, some of the other types of intermittent fasting were actually just variations of the 5:2 diet. There is also a 4:3 diet which sets three fasting days for every week; and 6:1 diet which only involves one fasting day in a week. If you don't find yourself fit to practice fasting for two days every week, then you can try some of these variations. As long as you stick to cutting your calorie intake into 25% during fasting periods, there shouldn't be any problem.

Eat-Stop-Eat Diet Plan

The eat-stop-eat diet plan was created by weight-loss expert Brad Pilon based on the concept of intermittent fasting. Pilon has a background in sports nutrition and supplements that is why this specific diet plan, according to diet experts, is more suitable for people who are usually involved in physical activities or sports.

In an eat-stop-eat diet plan, you fast for full 24 hours once or twice a week; thus, it is also called the 24-hour fast plan. Similar to 5:2 diet, you may eat normally during your non-fasting days. However, if both the consecutive and non-consecutive fast days are acceptable in 5:2 diet, in eat-stop-eat diet plan, only the non-consecutive days are deemed appropriate. In fact,

Pilon even expressly emphasized that one should not fast for consecutive days and neither should one fast for more than 48 hours in a single week.

There are no quantified calorie limits during fast days in this type of intermittent fasting; as you should aim for a complete abstinence from food if you are following eat-stop-eat diet. You can, however, take diet soda, sparkling water, tea, or coffee during such period. If you felt the need to break the full fast, Pilon says that you can eat whatever you want to eat but he also suggests that you moderate your consumption. Also, if you cannot fast for 24 hours straight, shorter periods will also work as long as it is not less than 20 hours.

After the 24-hour fast, it is advised that appropriate amount of calorie intake per day should be taken—approximately 2000 calories for women and 2500 calories for men. Also, high-quality protein is highly recommended in this diet. You may take 20 to 30 grams of it every four to five hours for a total of 100 grams per day. This is to ensure that lean muscle mass is retained during intermittent fasting.

Say, if you started your fast at 8 am on Tuesday, you can resume eating normally at 8 am on Wednesday. During the fasting period, starting at 8 am on Tuesday, you may drink coffee or diet soda and consume a total of 100 grams of high-quality protein. If you still find it hard to go through the day without eating meals, you may eat a little but make sure to limit it otherwise it cannot be considered as a fasting period. You can have your breakfast exactly at 8 am in the next morning as the fasting period ends at that time. You can go back to eating normally and after several non-fasting days, you can then repeat the 24-hour fast.

Remember, your fasting days should not be near to each other for this kind of plan not only is after weight loss but is also aiming to maintain lean muscle mass. Pilon also does not recommend pairing this diet schedule with low-carb meals as this will only result into energy deficiency. Individuals who adopt this type of intermittent fasting need appropriate levels of energy; hence, appropriate amount of glucose. This is also the reason that Pilon recommends taking the right amount of calorie intake per non-fasting day. The results of this diet plan are enhanced by consumption of fruits and vegetables.

16:8 Protocol

This intermittent fasting variant was originated by personal trainer and nutritional expert Martin Berkhan. Unlike the first two mentioned diet plans, this is a day-based fasting; which means that a cycle takes only a day to repeat and that each day is split into fasting and eating hours. 16:8 simply means a day should be composed of 16 hours of fasting and 8 hours of free-eating. The diet plan is known for its effectiveness not only to weight loss but also to lean mass gain, that's why Berkhan calls it the "leangains" method. You'll find out more about this type of intermittent fasting on the part II of this book.

The Warrior Diet

Ever imagined a Viking devouring a whole table of foods? What about a Spartan gulping a big barrel of wine? Well, one of these days, you might find yourself looking like these men as you take your meal under the Warrior Diet plan.

The Warrior Diet is one of the most popular diet plans that incorporate intermittent fasting. There is actually a whole book discussing about this and it was written by nutritional and fitness expert Ori Hofmekler, who apparently started this kind of diet philosophy. Hofmekler is the founder of Defense Nutrition. He has already authored a number of books to date, all of which tackle health and fitness.

So, how is Warrior Diet done? The diet plan essentially follows a day-based intermittent fasting schedule. On each day, you have to fast for 20 hours straight and eat at least once during the remaining four hours. The fasting period of 20 hours might sound like an uphill battle to some, considering it must be applied every—single—day; but don't worry, the fasting period in this diet protocol allows consumption of minimal servings of raw fruits and veggies, or a glass of fresh juice. You may also take small servings of protein if you want. Just don't eat a full-course meal during fast.

Fasting and eating periods under this diet pattern are more appropriately termed as "undereating" and "overeating" periods, respectively. So, we can say that the undereating phase is really intended for you to still be able to consume foods although such consumption must strictly be observed and limited. Overeating phase, on the other hand, is the four-hour period where you can eat tons of foods covering as many nutrients as possible. It is also important to set the overeating phase at night time.

For example, if you choose to set your overeating phase at six o'clock to ten o'clock in the evening, you must limit your food intake from 10 pm of the same night to 6 pm of the next day. During your 20-hour undereating phase you may take a small plate of pure vegetable salad or drink freshly extracted fruit or vegetable juice. You can also add a bit of protein to your salad by putting a few strips of lean chicken meat to it. Once the clock turns to 6 pm, you can now "overeat" as pointedly instructed by the diet plan. You may eat a large meal composed of a bowl of Caesar salad, a plate of steak and seared salmon, as well as a dish of carbonara or a clubhouse sandwich if you want to. Yes, this diet plan does mean it when it says to eat "tons" of foods. Besides, it isn't called Warrior Diet for nothing.

Speaking of being a "warrior" in this diet plan, you also need to discipline yourself like one. The diet protocol does not just instruct eating a lot during the four-hour overeating phase, it also highly recommends proper sequence of food intake once you start with your free-eating period. The order of food intake from first to last should be: vegetables, protein, fat, and carbohydrates. The first three should as much as possible be strictly taken in order. You may omit the carbohydrates if you want but you'd most likely need to eat some, considering this comes after a long period of fasting. The carbs are neither limited anyway so you can take as much as you want as long as they come after the veggies, protein, and fat.

The science behind this diet plan is a bit complex to explain. Contrary to the common diet rule that one should not eat late at night, as such will only result to weight gain, the philosophy that backs up this diet plan is linked to a different theory—humans are inherently nocturnal eaters. But despite holding on to a different view, nutrition experts are convinced with the protocol's effects in the body.

To explain, the undereating phase is meant to maximize "fight or flight" response of the sympathetic nervous system. Fight-or-flight response is a reaction made by the body in response to a perceived threat. Threat includes harmful events, imminent danger, or even survival threats like hunger. And since the body struggles with hunger during the 20-hour fast, the fight-or-flight responds by making the body more alert and boosting the energy which would eventually result to stimulating the fat burning process.

The overeating phase, on the other hand, is supposed to utilize the ability of the Parasympathetic Nervous System to promote digestion, as well as relaxation within the body. This allows the body to absorb the consumed nutrients and use it for repair and growth. It also helps the body burn fats during the day.

The benefits of Warrior Diet to the body will only be maximized if one follows the plan accordingly. Majority of those who tried this diet plan claim that this is a tough job to take. But at the end of the day, being able to witness the progress in your body is what matters the most. After all, it's a diet plan for the devoted and disciplined individuals—for the warriors-in-training.

Alternate-Day Fasting

Alternate-day fasting or up-day-down-day diet is a fasting protocol that follows a two-day cycle. It originated from the book UpDayDownDay Diet™ which was authored by plastic surgeon Dr. James Johnson. Doctor Johnson also struggled with weight loss himself, which led him to the discovery of an eating plan effective for weight loss.

The diet plan is fairly plain; you eat minimal servings of meals one day and you eat your usual servings the next day. In here, the days when you eat small or limited servings are called "down days" while those which allow you to consume normal servings are called "up days." The process simply repeats every two days and since it's a two-day cycle, there are really no particular days which can be set as either up days or down days (if your Monday this week is a down day then your Monday next week won't be the same assuming you followed the fasting schedule throughout the week).

The plan also entails a quantified limit of calorie intake that should be followed on down days as much as possible. It instructs that you only consume one fifth of your usual calorie intake during your down days. Therefore, if your normal consumption is approximately 2000 calories per day, then you should only take approximately 400 calories on your down days. Your down days would typically comprise regular or normal meals although those must come in smaller servings.

According to Doctor Johnson, if you find it hard to stick to your down days, you may opt for protein and calorie shakes or meal replacement shakes. These shakes are packed with essential nutrients and can safely substitute meals. However, these shakes are merely a help for you to survive down days especially when you are a beginner to this. They should only be taken on your first two weeks under this diet schedule and should not be a regular substitute for your meals every down day. After at most, two weeks, you should go back to eating "real" foods or meals so your body won't get used to depending on liquids and shakes.

If you are a gym rat, you might want to consider hitting the gym only on your up days, as these are the days on which you can surely sustain endurance on physical activities without breaking the diet plan. Lifting weights and engaging to other strenuous activities require quite a pack of energy and you can only have a decent amount of it on days when you eat "normal" or "enough" servings. Besides, alternate-day fasting is designed solely to promote weight loss. Trying to gain lean muscle mass while under this diet plan would entail additional efforts and those include disciplining your gym-enthusiast-self to rest on down days (and probably to eat more protein-rich servings).

Fat Loss Forever

If you're torn between the flexibility of eat-stop-eat diet and the free-eating feature of Warrior Diet, Fat Loss Forever diet might be the one that you're looking for. The diet plan was conceptualized by fitness expert John Romaniello and was made for gym-goers who want a flexible diet schedule that also includes the most important day of the week—cheat day.

The name "Fat Loss Forever" is actually a fancy title for a diet plan with a complicated mixture of different fasting protocols in one schedule. Unless you pull off the diet schedule properly, the "fat loss" is not going to come and the possibility that the fat will be lost "forever" won't be guaranteed. Nevertheless, it's still labeled as one of the most effective diet plans anchored to the concept of intermittent fasting.

The diet plan is essentially a week-based intermittent fasting and each week should include two primary periods: the cheat day and the 36-hour fast. The 36-hour fast should always come after the cheat day. After that, you should incorporate one or more intermittent fasting protocols for the rest of the week. Romaniello suggests that you save your 36-hour fast for the busiest days of your week so you'd be focused on more important things (e.g. work) other than your hunger.

Let's say, if you started your cheat day on Thursday at 8 am and ate your last "cheat" meal for the day at 9 pm, your 36-hour fast should start at 9 pm on the same day. Counting 36 hours from 9 pm, your next "normal meal" should be on Saturday at 9 am. That is indeed a long period of fast but of course, you can consume small servings of protein, carbs, fruits, and vegetables during the 36-hour period; just make sure you are not taking any full-course meal. Afterwards, if you decided to adopt alternate-day fasting for the rest of the week, then the day after your 36-hour fast (Saturday in this case) should be an up day as your body needs to recover enough nutrients after the fast. The next day which is Sunday, should then be a down day. The remaining days before the next Thursday should just be an alternating series of up and down days.

It is important to apply the corresponding rules under the different fasting protocols that you use for the rest of the week, after the cheat day and 36-hour fast. From the illustration above, your down days should only comprise one fifth of your average calorie consumption. If you happen to consume an average of approximately 2500 calories a day, you should limit your Sunday and Tuesday meals at 500 calories (one fifth of 2500) for the whole day.

For another example, let's say you started your cheat day on Sunday from 9 am to 10 pm. This sets your 36-hour fasting period at 10 pm on Sunday and from that, the period should end at 10 am on Tuesday. If you use the Warrior Diet for the rest of the week, then that forces you to extend the 36-hour fasting period to 44 to 48 hours. This is because the Warrior Diet follows a night-time eating schedule; and since your 36-hour fasting period ends at morning, you'll need to wait for another couple of hours before you can eat. Therefore, your next large meal should be on Tuesday around 6 or 8 pm. For Wednesday up to Saturday, the night-time eating rule shall also be applied accordingly. You can have your cheat day once again when the next Sunday arrives.

With regard to cheat days, it is crucial that you know what to eat when you are given such heavenly freedom. On these days, cakes, ice cream, sodas, fast foods, junk foods, or charred meats might be enticing but are they really worth it? Well, considering that you sacrificed probably the majority of your week in the name of fasting, those are more or less fine to eat (it's a cheat day anyway). You deserve them!

However, it will be a lot better if you focus on eating the healthier foods which offer all the nutrients that you were deprived of during the past few days of struggle. You fasted, so you technically did not just lose fats; some essential nutrients were also lost along the way. At least try to eat a lot of vegetables, fruits, lean meats, and healthy amount of fats and carbs first before taking the not-so-healthy second options. Also, do not forget the fact that anything taken excessively has corresponding undesirable effects.

The diet might seem so complicated at first but once you and your body get used to it, you'll find out that it's actually a rewarding diet plan. Plus, your body will also be able to flexibly adapt to changes as you switch from one diet protocol to another in order to fit in with your ever-changing personal schedule. Just stick to the two important parts of the week namely, the cheat day and the 36-hour fasting period; and let the rest of the week adapt to whatever intermittent fasting plans you decide to use.

Part II – Comprehensive Guide to Intermittent Fasting

CHAPTER 6

Taking the Action

If you already feel, by now, that you're ready to take the action and start implementing intermittent fasting to your daily life, you might want to consider to take it easy. Not that being excited is bad, though. It's just that, this is one of those points in your life when you should stop your happily excited spirit from rushing things out. Why?

A lot of people fail to realize that just because you have already learned the basics and foundational concepts of intermittent fasting, doesn't mean you are fully ready to apply it in your life. Those who failed with their diet plans most probably overlooked something that could've otherwise made their weight-loss journey successful—preparation.

Reading about fasting is different from actually doing it. It's easier said than done. Therefore, preparation must come in between reading and practicing. And to help you with your preparation, you may consider the following order of guidelines: self-assessment, choosing a diet plan, understanding the importance of exercise, and learning about the fasting foods and liquids.

Assessing Yourself

First things first—are you ready? In intermittent fasting, being ready doesn't just refer to your body's capability to undergo sets of fasting periods; it also refers to your mental state of readiness. Being physically ready to intermittent fasting is generally easy. The human body can inherently last even up to two weeks without food. So, the real question would be, are you mentally ready?

You need to assess yourself as early as now because if you are not mentally ready, chances are you'll end up breaking your fasting rules, ditching your fasting periods, disregarding your diet, giving in to temptations, or worse, losing your motivation halfway. The reason you need to assess yourself is that you'll be sacrificing time and effort for this matter, and you probably wouldn't want to spend significant amounts of these two precious things just to find out that you don't want to continue with your diet plan anymore.

If you are, however, sure that you are ready for a change in your lifestyle and that you can take or endure whatever it may bring, then you can expect that everything else that follows after this first stage of preparation would be easy for you.

Choosing a Diet Plan

The worst part about choosing a diet plan, most especially if you are a beginner, is that you are not sure whether your chosen plan will be successful or not; and that it takes at least a month before you can say if you made the right choice or not. The truth is, each and every type of intermittent fasting diet plan entails a risk of failure and that there's no such thing as a "perfect" diet plan that can absolutely guarantee either weight loss or muscle mass gain, not even among the most prominent ones listed in the previous chapter.

There is, however, a measure that can help you minimize the risk of failing with a diet program; we'll call it personal filtering. Personal filtering simply means that you filter out, among the options you have, the one which best suits your preferences. It's a pre-implementation analysis that identifies which among the option, prior to its implementation, could provide the most positive outcome by examining the features of each available option. The main idea is to remove as many options as possible from the choices you have until you come up with, most preferably, one option which will then be deemed as fit for you.

To demonstrate, let's try to use the types of intermittent fasting given in the previous chapter (except for the 16:8 protocol since it was not yet discussed thoroughly). The first eliminating question should be, "what is your goal?" Are you after weight loss? Muscle gain? Or both? Assuming you are after both, then that already removes Fat Loss Forever Diet from the list since it's designed solely for weight loss. Next question would be, "how much fasting can you endure?" The question can be answered as a number of hours per day or a number of days per week. Suppose that your work schedule only permits fasting for a maximum of two days a week. This cancels out The Warrior Diet and the Alternate-day fasting from your choices as both require more than two days of fasting in a single week.

You now have narrowed down your choices into two: the 5:2 diet and the Eat-Stop-Eat diet. The deciding factor should now be based on the differences between the two. The 5:2 diet is a more flexible than Eat-Stop-Eat as you can fast for either two straight consecutive days or two non-consecutive days. It is also good if you only want to limit your consumption during fasting days rather than to completely abstain from it. Plus, it goes with a quantified limit (25% of your average daily calorie intake) so in case you feel like you're going beyond limit you can just check it through computation.

Eat-stop-eat on the other hand, best suits the sports and gym enthusiasts as such diet plan is specifically made for them. If you are seriously devoted to fasting, this is also a better choice since the goal in each fasting day is full abstinence. Now, assuming you are a sports enthusiast whose desire to lose weight and gain muscle mass is at peak, then your final choice would obviously be the Eat-stop-eat Diet.

It is important to remember that personal filtering is merely a guide to help you choose the most appropriate diet plan for you. It does not guarantee success although it can be inferred that it somehow increases your chance to succeed since through it, you'll be able to choose the diet program which can be implemented in accordance to your schedule and needs.

Recognizing Exercise as an Important Factor to Weight Loss

If your ultimate goal for using intermittent fasting is to shed pounds, then from now on, you must see weight-loss exercises as your biggest friend. It is true that intermittent fasting alone can burn your fats and provide evident results; but pairing it with proper exercise, you'll cut the progress time almost into half. Yes, with proper guidance and consistent dedication, these rather exhausting activities could accelerate the results.

Of course, if you are new to diet plans and intermittent fasting, you do not have to engage immediately on physical exercise. Let your body adapt to the changes first and when you feel like it already has, you can start by choosing which set of exercises is suitable for your physique, for your endurance, and most importantly, for your diet program.

Learning About Fasting Foods and Liquids

Pre-familiarizing yourself with the foods and drinks you can take during partially restricted fasting periods is also important. It's because most of the diet plans under intermittent fasting allow consumption of minimal servings of foods during fast hours or days. In general, foods that are considered safe during fasts include vegetables and fruits, whole grains, low-fat and low-sodium foods.

Liquids on the other hand are usually more available and safer during fasts. Water and fresh juices are typically recommended when you are under intermittent fasting. Protein or meal replacement shakes are also used in some techniques. Smoothies, juices, and shakes that are made up of nutrients-rich ingredients are also advised to be taken.

If you want to know the particular options you have, there is a list provided on the latter part of the book that enumerates specific fasting foods and liquids you can take during partially restricted fasting periods.

It must be emphasized that the measures above are mere guidelines for you to maximize the potential results of any weight-loss program that you decide to implement in your lifestyle. They do not guarantee perfect outcomes. The only key to make sure that a diet plan is going to provide desirable results is strict adherence. Honestly, all of these diet plans are programmed to work but unless you follow them correctly, you can never achieve optimum results. Temptations and frustrations already await you the moment you take your first step to your weight-loss journey. So, let me ask you the question once again—are you ready?

CHAPTER 7

The Beginner's Protocol

By now you should have assessed yourself and have also decided that you are going to openly welcome intermittent fasting to your life—that's the spirit! And assuming you are indeed done with the self-assessment process, let's now proceed to the second step which is choosing the best type of intermittent fasting-based diet plan.

Whether you are new exclusively to intermittent fasting or completely new to diet plans in general, there's one type of intermittent fasting that would likely fit your current lifestyle, and would only incur little changes in your daily life once implemented. If you are, however, neither of the two, don't worry because this diet plan is also suitable to everyone else, even if you are a healthy person of normal weight. The diet plan is called the 16:8 method.

16:8 Method - How It Is Done

As once explained in chapter 5, this diet plan was introduced by personal trainer and nutritional expert Martin Berkhan. It's a daily intermittent fasting which divides each day into 16 hours of fasting period and 8 hours of normal- or free-eating period. The original term for this method was "Leangains method" as referred to by Berkhan but the term "16:8 method" is kind of getting more and more popular than the former. In this book, we'll also refer to it as the beginner's protocol.

The first thing to consider in 16:8 protocol is on which part of the day should both the fasting and eating periods be set. Fortunately, there exists a "standard" setting for both periods so you might want to just adopt it since it has already been tested and proven by the majority of 16:8 diet plan followers. Under the said setting, the 16-hour fasting period runs from 8 pm one day to 12 pm or 12 noon the next day. This means that, in a single day, you can only eat from 12 pm to 8 pm.

Such standardized setting is not really that hard to implement. Come to think of it, a dinner at let's say, 7:30 pm is quite an appropriate time considering that you are most probably in a fat-loss diet. It's not too early which means your body can sustain hunger before sleeping time; and neither is it too late which means proper digestion can still be expected.

There are no restrictions with regard to the meals that you can take during the eight-hour eating window; thus, you can eat normal meals at normal servings. Most of the people who practice the 16:8 method, however, cuts the number of meals they take into two. They usually skip breakfast since the eating window starts at lunch time anyway. Nonetheless, you can still stick to taking three regular-sized meals a day if you want to, as long as you take all three within the eating window.

The schedule simply repeats every day. You can expect your first few days or weeks to be burdensome but once your body adapts to the cycle, you'll get used to it and most importantly, you'll start to notice the progress.

Benefits of 16:8 Method

- Increased Chances of Fat Loss

Since your body's metabolism becomes slower as it enters the sleeping state, it naturally functions slower at night. Therefore, anything that is consumed beyond 8 pm to 9 pm, or at any time near bed time, won't likely be burned properly. This is the reason 16:8 method is a top choice when it comes to weight loss. It limits the chances of calories getting stored as fats by setting the dinner or last meal for the day, at an earlier and safer hour. And because the body is most probably secured from obtaining unwanted increase in fat mass, it'll be easier to lose weight.

- Lean Mass Retention

The body weight comprises two major composition namely, fat mass and lean mass. Therefore, when we say "weight loss," it can refer to the loss of either fat mass or lean mass; but most of the time, both. The ideal result, however, is to lose fat mass but not lean mass. Lean mass is important as it includes muscle mass which certainly needs to be maintained as much as possible, to keep your muscle strength at an optimal level. Fortunately, 16:8 method promotes retention of much of the lean mass in the body amid significant reduction in fat mass.

- Controlled Hunger

In 16:8 diet plan, your eating window is narrowed down to an eight-hour period. This eventually leads to changes in your body's natural cravings. Of course, you won't notice the effect on your first few weeks under the diet plan; but if you continue to commit yourself to the plan, your body will start to "reprogram" itself and get used to not feeling much of the usual, stubbornly constant hunger. Plus, it'll also be easier for you to get satisfied with meals.

- Improved Insulin Response

An improved insulin response is a contributory factor to both the lean mass retention and the controlled hunger mentioned above. But aside from that, it also makes insulin levels more stable that's why some of the people who are at risk of diabetes type 2 devotedly follow 16:8 method.

- Enhanced Brain Function

If you're stressing about not being able to think properly while fasted, then let 16:8 method cut your worries. On your first few days under 16:8 method, your brain will probably not function well as it's still trying to adapt to certain changes. But once it has, you'll notice that your mentality can function just as normally as it could before intermittent fasting—or even better. This is because your body is not forced to pump large amount of blood to your digestive system when you are fasted. Thus, it's able to deliver more oxygen to other parts including your brain.

Constructing Your Own 16:8 Schedule

For most people, especially to beginners, it's highly advised to implement 16:8 diet using the standard, 12 pm to 8 pm eating-window schedule. However, if your personal schedule does not permit such setting or you simply don't want to follow the norm, then you can schedule your own plan to fit your lifestyle.

The first question to ask here is which among the three major meals is going to be eliminated? The answer will either be based on your schedule or be coming from your own preference although you should also consider the importance of each meal to your weight-loss goal. Putting that in mind, it would be best for you to skip dinner. If it's impossible, however, your second-best choice would be eliminating breakfast so as to make sure that any excess on your dinner intake still has time to be burned in the morning. Lunch is the most unlikely to be eliminated since the meals that you consume on your lunch time are more or less burned properly regardless if you are under a diet plan or not.

Say, for example, your work starts at 8 am and ends at 3 pm, your best option would be skipping dinner, as it is the time of the day when much, if not all, of your work is probably done; hence, no hunger-triggering activity. Skipping breakfast might be dangerous when you are a complete beginner to fasting. So, for such situation, you may start your eating window at 7:30 am to 3:30 pm. Within such window, you can eat your breakfast at 7:30 am or 7:45 am, before you go to work; and have your last meal right exactly at 3 pm, after work or a little later at 3:30 pm. Addition of an in-between meal is not much of an issue here so you can have lunch at 11 am or 12 pm and still eat some more after work as long as it's covered by the eating window.

If you can, however, endure a no-breakfast morning even at work, you can move the beginning of your eating window to 11 am to 12 pm or exactly to your lunch break. If your lunch break starts at 11 am, then you can eat your lunch at 11 am and adjust your last meal time to 7 pm, or to any time earlier than that. If you get used to this setting, you'll find out that it's actually easier and better to skip breakfast as you can expect an increase in focus and other brain functions as previously explained in the benefits of 16:8 method.

Your eating-window also does not necessarily have to be a full eight-hour period. You may further narrow it down into seven or four hours. However, such is only advisable if you have been using intermittent fasting for a long period of time. If you are still beginning to adapt to the lifestyle, then sticking to an eight-hour eating window is strongly recommended.

Cheat Days - to Cheat or Not to Cheat?

16:8 method is not a religious devotion so you can start celebrating because apparently, cheat day is allowed under this diet schedule. Some of the followers of the diet plan claimed that they've still succeeded losing significant weight even if they admittedly cheated for a couple of days in some of the weeks. The safest number of cheat days you can have per week is one; but it's not a hard and fast rule so you can have your cheat days for two or three days a week. Just make sure that majority of the days in your week still follow the 16:8 plan, especially if you really are into achieving weight loss.

Also, it would be better not to overeat on your cheat days. A cheat day only means that you can extend your eating-window for more than eight hours or you can simply break the fasting period; but it does not mean that you should eat a lot of sweets and fatty foods every hour. Always eat in moderation whether it involves a healthy or unhealthy food. The result of 16:8 diet plan largely depends on you so always consider that.

Famous People with 16/8-Diet-Bodies

Actor Hugh Jackman, majorly known for playing the role of Wolverine in the X-men movies, is one of the most prominent Hollywood figures to date. The actor has always been a center of interest to diet experts and fitness magazines for his ripped, Wolverine physique which Jackman proudly claims to be the result of his 16:8 diet schedule. At least now you know that the secret to Wolverine's size and strength is not found on his mutant genes—but to 16:8 diet.

Another popular actor who uses 16:8 diet plan is Terry Crews. He explained that his eating-window goes from 2 pm to 10 pm and he fasts for the rest of the day. He also does not eat foods, even minimal amounts of it during fasts, although he drinks coffee or tea during such periods. According to Crews, the only problem with 16:8 method is that you don't want a "bad meal" for your eating period because no one waits for 16 hours just to end up eating a bad meal.

David Kingsburry, trainer of some celebrities including Chris Hemsworth, Michael Fassbender, and Jennifer Lawrence, also promotes the 16:8 diet plan because aside from its effectiveness, the schedule, as Kingsburry said, can easily fit in an individual's lifestyle.

CHAPTER 8

The Complementary Guide

After choosing the intermittent fasting diet plan, the guidelines state that the next two things to consider would be: learning about exercise and getting familiar with fasting foods and liquids. The first thing you need to know about these two is that they are both supplemental factors to intermittent fasting and are meant to help you maximize results.

Guide to Exercises

What's better than acquiring the weight-loss benefit of the beginner's protocol is maximizing the lean mass retention it features. It would be easier to gain muscle mass while under the diet plan since, as once mentioned earlier, much of the lean mass is retained despite weight loss. But if you are only after the weight loss, then that's equally fine. In any case, it's important that you utilize your 16-hour fasting window for many positive things can happen within that period of time.

The ideal time to apply weight-loss exercises while under intermittent fasting would be during the fasted period, most preferably in the morning. Considering you skip breakfasts during your 16-hour fasts, a complete exercise in the morning can burn significant amount of fats in your body. Provided below is a list of some of the well-known exercises that you may do every morning, to help accelerate the fat burning process and maintain your weight-loss progress:

- Squats
- Lunges (including explosive lunges)
- Kettlebell Swings
- Tabata Drill
- Double Jump
- Body-Weight Exercises
- Burpees

- Mountain Climbers

- Jump Rope

Guide to Training and Workout

Guidelines for strength training and muscle workouts are essentially stricter than weight-loss exercises. This is because in the latter, the only goal is to lose weight while in the former, the objective is to gain muscle mass while losing weight at the same time.

Training or workout may be done either during a fasted period or within an eating window. If you cannot commit to a fasted training, then it would be more appropriate if you train or work out in the middle of your eating window. In such case, you have to secure three meals within your eating window to support your system.

To illustrate, assume for example that you adopted the standard 16:8 schedule. This means that your workout shall be within the eating window, 12 pm to 8 pm. Your 12-noon lunch shall serve as your pre-workout meal. It must comprise 20-25% of your daily calorie intake. After that, your training should be set around 3:30 to 4:00 pm (it is important that the training is set at least an hour after pre-workout meal). Assuming the training takes an hour, your post-workout meal should be around 4:30 to 5:00 pm. Your post-workout meal should always be the largest meal. You should then take your dinner or the last meal of the day at either 7:00 pm or 8:00 pm to help you sustain the following fasting period.

It is also possible that you take two pre-workout meals before working out. Let's use one of the examples we had last chapter (eating window at 7:30 am to 3:30 pm) for demonstration. Your breakfast at 7:30 am should serve as your first pre-workout meal. Your next meal, let's say at 11:30 am, should then be your second pre-workout meal. Each of your pre-workout meals should consist 20-25% of your daily calorie consumption. Counting a few hours from your second pre-workout meal, you may start your training at 2:30 pm. Assuming again that your training takes only an hour, your post-workout, and last meal for the day should be taken exactly at 3:30 pm.

Now for the fasted training, you should first familiarize yourself with the branched-chain amino acids or BCAAs. These are amino acids usually taken, in the form of tablets or powder, to stimulate protein synthesis especially during trainings or workouts. Protein synthesis is essential for muscle growth and stimulating it serves as a defense against protein breakdown.

For a workout day, it is strongly recommended that you ready three 10-gram BCAA tablets or a 30-gram BCAA powder. The BCAA supplements will be used throughout a portion your fasted period. You should take one 10-gram BCAA tablet after your pre-workout. Afterward, you can proceed to your workout. Take another tablet an hour after your workout and take the last one two hours after your last intake. If you are going to use the powder, simply mix it in a shake or in a drink and divide the whole drink into three equal servings.

To demonstrate using the standard schedule, if you wake up at 6 am, your first tablet shall be taken after a five- to fifteen-minute pre-workout. Your training shall then start at 7 am and end at 8 am assuming it's a one-hour training. You shall take the second tablet around 8 am, right after the training. The last tablet shall then be taken at 10 am, two hours after the last intake.

Your lunch at 12 pm should serve as your post-workout meal; hence, the largest meal of the day. Your dinner or last meal should normally be taken at 8 pm. It's up to you if you want to consume in-between meals. If you commit to this strategy, your body will gain more muscle strength and will only lose fat mass in the process.

Guide to 16:8 Diet-Specific Fasting Foods and Liquids

There are no fasting foods that are labeled safe to be consumed during the 16-hour period. To be honest, the fasting period in beginner's protocol is not much of a burden if you compare it to other fasting periods; like the 20-hour fast in Warrior Diet or the two-day fast under 5:2 Diet. Therefore, fasting foods aren't really an ultimate necessity. And the only means available to ease your 16-hour struggle are gums and fasting liquids.

Gums are good for people who often confuse boredom with hunger. If you're bored and you feel like the only answer to it is food, then try chewing a gum. Sometimes, you're not really craving for a food but instead, you just want to chew something in your mouth. The gum, however, that is referred to in this guide is a sugar-free gum. Sweeteners on regular chewing gums will only break your fast so you should avoid them.

In terms of fasting liquids, you can drink water if you want. As a matter of fact, you should drink a lot of it during fast. It does not only improve your metabolism but it also helps suppress hunger. Detox water, is also counted and is actually more preferable. Try adding a mint leaf or a slice of lemon to each glass to obtain better and more refreshing effects.

Black coffee and green tea can also save you from your fasting struggles most especially during the morning. They can help increase fat burning process and delay hunger. These beverages, however, should not come with large amounts of milk and sugar.

Take note that all of these are specifically applicable only to 16:8 diet protocol. Some diet plans do not allow most or all of the foods and drinks stated above, while some allow a wider range of options. If you want to learn more about the general fasting foods and liquids that are allowed under most of intermittent fasting-based diet plans, you can check the list provided in the next chapter.

Part III – Supplemental Section

CHAPTER 9

Fasting Foods and Liquids

Contrary to the traditional fasting that refers to absolute abstinence from foods and liquids, intermittent fasting refers to a period where one's consumption is limited only to some fasting specifications. The limits among diet plans slightly vary depending on which type of intermittent fasting you opted to follow. Nevertheless, there are specific foods and liquids that are generally present and allowed in almost any type of diet plan.

Fruits and Vegetables

The tandem always tops almost any list of ideal foods that must be eaten for a healthier life. This is obviously because fruits and vegetables are legitimate sources of vitamins and minerals. Plus, they are naturally high in antioxidants. You can eat a serving or two of either a fruit salad or vegetable salad during your partially restricted fasting period. Or you can just directly eat a raw fruit or veggie for convenience. Below is a list of the most recommended fruits that you may consume during fasted periods:

- Green Apples
- Strawberries
- Oranges
- Blackberries
- Cranberries
- Grapefruit
- Papaya
- Cantaloupes
- Raisins

- Apricots
- Guava

Roughly speaking, any vegetable, as long as it's not canned, is fairly good during fasted periods. However, there are vegetables which pack a particular combination of nutrients fit for an empty stomach; hence, perfect for fasting periods. Some of these vegetables are:

- Spinach
- Mustard Greens
- Cauliflower
- Brussels Sprouts
- Tomatoes
- Kale
- Lettuce
- Broccoli
- Cabbage
- Bok Choy
- Swiss Chard

Take note that the available fruits and vegetables appropriate for your fasting periods are not limited to the lists given above. Those just list the most recommended ones as they contain the vitamins and minerals that your body specially needs during fasted state. You have several more choices beyond those included in the list.

Nuts

In some intermittent fasting variants, foods which contain fats are allowed, and even suggested, to be consumed during fasted periods. So, to ensure that you are getting only the healthy fats, you can opt to go with nuts. Nuts contain both monounsaturated and polyunsaturated fats. These fats are also known as the good fats.

Good fats are "good" because they help lower your risk of stroke and other heart diseases and they also help lower cholesterol levels. Furthermore, they also contain omega-3 fatty acids, fiber, L-arginine, and vitamin E, all of which are known for being heart-friendly substances. The healthiest nuts that you can eat during fasting period are listed below:

- Brazil Nuts
- Macadamia Nuts
- Cashews
- Pecans
- Pine Nuts
- Walnuts
- Almonds
- Chestnuts
- Pistachios

Of course, nuts during fasting periods should be limited accordingly to what your specific diet plan allows. The main reason they are fine to eat during fasted state is that they satisfy the body almost the same way as meats do. Therefore, they can somehow extend your body's endurance to hunger. Their benefits, especially to the heart, are also considered as a contributory factor.

Soups

If you want to spend your fasted period eating something with a meaty taste but your diet plan only allows liquid, then the best option you have is a soup. Soups are easily digested by the body so it can be safely taken without worrying about breaking the fast. The ideal number of servings for a soup during a fasted period is one; but taking two bowls of it won't hurt your fasting. Try to limit soup intake only up to two servings per fasting period. To name a few diet-friendly soups, we have:

- Vegetable Broth
- Spinach-Artichoke Soup
- Moroccan Stew
- Corn Chowder
- Black Bean Minestrone
- Lentil-Vegetable Soup
- Carrot and Ginger Soup

Protein and Meal Replacement Shakes

First on the list of fasting liquids are the protein and meal replacement shakes. Protein shakes are flavored shakes which contain large amounts of protein good for working out and training. Meal replacement shakes, on the other hand, contain almost similar substances except that they have lower protein content, but higher calorie content than protein shakes.

If the fasting periods under your specific diet plan limit meals into a certain number of calories per day, it will be best for you to substitute your meal with a meal replacement shake. Meal replacement shakes have quantifiable calorie amounts (e.g. 400 calories per glass) so it will be easier for you to track your calorie intake during fasted periods.

If you are more into training during your fasted days, going for protein shakes is a wise idea. A protein shake, with its massive protein content, can help support your muscle strength throughout and after training. Plus, measuring calorie intake with protein shakes is easy as well.

Detox Water

You can safely drink a detox water under any intermittent fasting plan. Detox water is simply a plain water with a bit of "detoxifying" agents in it, like mint leaves, orange slices, or cinnamon sticks. And since it combines the cleansing-benefit of water and the fat-burning, detoxifying properties of herbs or fruits, into one glass, it's pretty much a better option to drink than plain drinking water. You get to be cleansed and detoxified at the same time.

Fresh Juices and Smoothies

Making a smoothie or juice out of fruits or vegetables is a common practice among people who couldn't stand a fasting period without sipping a refreshing flavored drink. There are no specifications about which flavors of juices and smoothies must be drunk. As long as a juice or smoothie is made from fresh, raw, and organic fruits and vegetables, a glass or two of the drink is perfectly fine.

Coffees and Teas

Teas are more flexible in fasting than coffees. You can drink a cup of jasmine tea, green tea, or any tea during fasted periods. Teas contain few calories and they won't derail your fasting protocol. They can also be served either hot or cold but a hot tea is more preferred by most.

On the other hand, only black coffees are allowed during fasted periods. It is also advised not buy coffees from coffee shops, as they roughly contain excessive amount of artificial sweetener, and high-fat creamers. If you want to add some sugar to your tea or coffee, you may do so as long as you limit such at regulated amounts.

CHAPTER 10

Recipes for the Hungry

You, and everyone else who follow any type of intermittent fasting will always have something in common—you're all at your hungriest a few minutes before the eating window starts. And you know what's better than being able to eat after a long period of starvation? The foods, themselves.

Your first and last meals (or perhaps any meal within the eating window) are considerably precious to you that's why there's really no space for—as Terry Crews calls it—a "bad meal." So, consider rewarding yourself every time you survive a fasting period and serve some of the best recipes that you'll discover in this section.

Fresh Mexican Tuna Salad

It's a Pico de Gallo-inspired tuna recipe which combines protein-packed tuna with fresh veggies. It's low in fat and carbohydrates so you can eat more servings of this recipe during your eating window. It's a good post-workout meal too!

Ingredients:

- 2 large tomatoes (chopped)
- 1 large red onion (chopped)
- 1 bunch of Chinese parsley (chopped)
- 1 400-gram can of Tuna (flakes, preferably)
- 1 pc. of lime

Number of Servings:

2 bowls

Directions:

To get rid of the onions' aftertaste, place the chopped onion in a bowl and liberally sprinkle salt on it. Pour a cup of water into the bowl or until the salted onions are all covered with water. Let them sit for half an hour or until the onions have soaked. Afterwards, drain the onions and rinse with running water to remove any excess salt.

In a large bowl, mix the chopped tomatoes, Chinese parsley, and the onion. Squeeze a piece of lime over the mixture. Drain the can of tuna and combine the flakes with the vegetables. Gently toss the ingredients and serve.

Grilled BBQ Chicken Flatbreads

Eating pizza while under a diet plan might sound like an unforgivable sin—but if it's a pizza in the form of grilled flatbreads then it's totally fine. The recipe is an ideal snack to pack your calorie-deprived body with some calories and protein after a fasting period. Plus, this provides portion-controlled servings so there is nothing to worry about overeating.

Ingredients:

- 2 flatbreads
- 12 ounces chicken breast (boneless and skinless)
- 2 slices chopped Canadian bacon
- 1 cup of sliced red onions
- 1 cup of sliced bell pepper (yellow or red)
- 1 tbsp. fresh pineapple juice
- 1/4 cup chopped pineapple tidbits
- 1/4 cup barbeque sauce*
- 1/4 cup grated cheese
- a pinch of black pepper

Number of Servings:

4 slices

Directions:

Preheat the grill at 500 °F. On a grill tray, place the sliced onions and bell peppers then sprinkle on some pepper. Coat the chicken breast with cooking spray. Bring the chicken and the onions and bell peppers to grill. Cook each side of the chicken for three to four minutes or until the inside reaches 165 °F. Remove the veggies and chicken from the grill and then reduce the heat to 400 °F.

Transfer the chicken on to a cutting board and cut into strips or bite-sized pieces. In a blender, add the pineapple juice and barbecue sauce and pulse until the combination forms a thick sauce.

Place the flatbreads on a pizza stone or screen. Spread half a cup of the sauce on each flatbread, and top with the chicken cuts, Canadian bacon, grated cheese, grilled onions and bell peppers, and pineapple tidbits; then place on the grill. Close the lid and wait for around 10 minutes to cook, or until the cheese has melted.

Remove from heat. Let the flatbread cool for a while before slicing; then serve.

Low-fat Chicken Spaghetti Carbonara

If you're a pasta lover then here's a simple recipe for you. This is specially made for people who devote themselves so much in a diet plan that they thought they are prohibited from indulging in dishes like Spaghetti Carbonara. But more importantly, this is made to complement low-fat diet plans.

Ingredients:

- 150 grams of pasta
- 1 skinless chicken breast (chopped)
- 4 short-cut lean bacon slices
- 2 cloves garlic (crushed)
- 1/2 onion (sliced)
- 2 spring onions (sliced)
- 1 tbsp. olive oil
- cracked pepper
- 3/4 cup light evaporative milk

Number of Servings:

2 plates

Directions:

Cook pasta as per instructions; then drain and set aside.

Preheat a non-stick fry-pan at medium heat. Add a little olive oil on the pan and cook bacon until crispy. Once the bacon becomes crispy, set it aside. Add a little olive oil again on the same pan then cook the onion on low heat until soft. Set the onion aside along with the bacon.

Add the remaining olive oil on the pan, turn to medium heat, and cook the chicken breast for around four to five minutes, until semi-cooked. Afterwards, slightly lower the heat and add the bacon and onion to the chicken, and then add garlic. Pour the evaporated milk then season with pepper to taste.

Stir the sauce occasionally while heating. Once the sauce bubbles, further lower the heat and add the cooked pasta. When the sauce turns into a slightly thick consistency, turn off the heat. Add the sliced spring onions then serve.

Green Tea Powerhouse Smoothie

There's no way that you won't look for a refreshing break after a heated struggle with your fasting period. And one of the best refreshments available for a conscious, weight-watcher is this antioxidant-rich smoothie recipe. Combine all the vitamins that your body would surely need after a fasting window and add a pack of protein to that—voila! A green tea powerhouse smoothie.

Ingredients:

- 1 bag of green tea
- ½ medium banana
- 1½ frozen blueberries
- ¾ light vanilla soy milk
- 3 tbsp. water
- 2 tsp. honey

Number of Servings:

1 glass

Directions:

Steam or microwave water in small bowl. Once steaming hot, add tea bag and let it brew for three to five minutes. Remove tea bag afterwards. Add honey and stir the mixture. In a blender, combine tea mixture, banana, blueberries, and soy milk. Blend on the highest setting. Transfer the smoothie into a glass and serve.

Protein-Packed Dark Choco-Almond Cookies

Dessert time is always more fun when you're not anxious about your weight and health. These cookies are going to bring your protein-diet gaming to the next level. Imagine being able to enjoy a delicious cookie while also gaining a dose of protein in every bite. It's a win-win situation, isn't it?

Ingredients:

- 1/4 cup unflavored protein powder
- 2 squares chopped dark chocolate (20 grams)
- 1/4 cup almonds (ground)
- 3 tbsp. almond butter
- 1/4 cup almond milk
- 1 tsp. coconut oil
- 2 tsp. coconut sugar

Number of Servings:

5 cookies

Directions:

Preheat oven to 350 °F. Mix protein powder, almonds, coconut sugar, almond butter, almond milk, and coconut oil together to make a dough. Once mixed, add dark chocolate. Roll dough into small-sized balls and place onto a tray lined with parchment paper. Flatten the balls with a spoon or with your fingers.

Place in the oven and bake for around 10 to 12 minutes or until baked. Remove from oven. Let the cookies rest to stiffen (and to prevent crumbling). Serve once completely cooled.

CONCLUSION

Perhaps, for the past centuries, people haven't found the ideal method of losing weight because we focused solely on the idea that what makes a person unhealthy or over-weight, is the kind of foods that he eats. Although it's legitimately true to some extent, it's not enough that we should focus only on a single idea and stop putting efforts to discover more from a different perspective.

Fortunately, intermittent fasting has been discovered right on the period when almost all of us are already giving up with our unsuccessful diet plans, brought by our desperate decisions—lots of thanks to the founders of the method!

And after reading all the chapters in this book, you have probably learned the important points about intermittent fasting. You discovered the method and learned about the science that, although is still being further proven by researchers across the globe, backs up much of the concept of the diet technique.

You also learned about the benefits of intermittent fasting not only to your weight but also to your overall health; from your insulin levels to your brain function. And above all, the method serves as a safer and even a better substitute to other diet plans as it has proven its purpose as a healthier way of losing weight and a bigger help to gaining muscle mass and strength.

You also know by now that there is a pool of options from which you can choose the type of intermittent fasting that best suits your lifestyle and needs. And if you can't decide on which among the options to choose, you can always go back to the book's comprehensive guide for beginners.

At this point, you already have everything you need to learn so you'd be able start your own journey to a healthy weight loss. Always remember that—regardless of the kind of diet plan that you implement, the outcome will always depend on your effort and most importantly, on your dedication. So, don't just do the process, commit yourself to it!

Thank you!

Before you go, I just wanted to say thank you for purchasing my book.

You could have picked from dozens of other books on the same topic but you took a chance and chose this one.

So, a HUGE thanks to you for getting this book and for reading all the way to the end.

Now I wanted to ask you for a small favor. **Could you please take just a few minutes to leave a review for this book on Amazon?**

This feedback will help me continue to write the type of books that will help you get the results you want. So if you enjoyed it, please let me know! (-:

www.ingramcontent.com/pod-product-compliance
Lightning Source LLC
Chambersburg PA
CBHW051752100526
44591CB00017B/2662